# THE 20% FACTOR

To Graham Tarrant

# THE
# 20%
# FACTOR

YOU • YOUR LIFE • YOUR SKILLS • YOUR JOB

IMMEDIATE ACHIEVABLE IMPROVEMENTS

## GRAHAM LANCASTER

LONDON   NEW YORK   SYDNEY   TORONTO

First published in 1993

This edition published 1993
by BCA by arrangement with
Kogan Page Ltd

CN 9845

Typeset by Saxon Graphics Ltd, Derby
Printed in England by Clays Ltd, St Ives plc.

'Under performers (which means nearly everybody) will take heart, wisdom and encouragement from Graham Lancaster's book which manages to entertain while instructing, and whose instructions could not be more to the point – that is for those with the will to succeed.'

**Robert Heller**
**The UK's leading management writer and former Editor-In-Chief,** *Management Today*

'Clearly displays the psychology and values underlying the author's undoubted success in the field of public relations.'

*The Director*

'Lancaster's book is full of useful hints.'

*Campaign*

'Outstandingly good', 'refreshingly different', 'highly readable and well informed'.

**British Institute of Management**

'....rugged individualism is out and conformity is in.'

*The Times*

# ABOUT THE AUTHOR

Graham Lancaster is Chairman and co-founder of Biss Lancaster plc, one of the UK's largest public relations consultancies, now owned by EURO RSCG, the largest communications group in Europe.

Born in Salford, Lancashire, Graham Lancaster began his career at 18 in production management with Hawker Siddeley Aviation and Corah, the Marks & Spencer knitwear supplier. He then joined the Confederation of British Industry where he remained for nearly seven years. As Policy Coordinator to the CBI President, he was in daily contact with UK and international business, trade union and political leaders.

He is a regular speaker at management conferences and is also highly experienced in TV and radio.

In addition to *The 20% Factor* he has written two spy thrillers – *The Nuclear Letters* (Methuen (UK), Atheneum (USA)) and *Seward's Folly* (Methuen) – which were also published in Germany. He has also had a number of short stories published in, for example, the *Sunday Telegraph* magazine, and has a regular column in *Haymarket's Marketing* magazine.

# CONTENTS

# ACKNOWLEDGEMENTS

I am grateful for the help of Dr David Lewis in the preparation of most of the self-analysis charts, and to Andrew Sargent. I also gratefully acknowledge permission to use a table from *Communicating in Organisations*, by Gerald M Phillips (Macmillan Publishing Company, New York, © 1982), and two tables from Norman R E Maier and Gertrude Casselman Verser's *Psychology in Industrial Organisations* (Fifth Edition, © 1982 Houghton Mifflin Company).

# INTRODUCTION

You can improve yourself in business and in your social life by 20% almost overnight. 20% greater salary, sales, profits, satisfaction, prospects of promotion and security are all there for the taking.

This is *The 20% Factor* that new management brooms, consultants, trainers, psychologists and other relative outsiders go for and generally deliver as part of their magic. Rapid improvements much beyond this are subject to the law of diminishing returns and depend on basic factors which need more fundamental attention or which are largely outside anyone's control.

This book is not concerned with the breathless pursuit of excellence. The constant flow of 'look at me, Ma' books from tycoons and consultants can seriously damage your confidence. Aiming for management superstar status is by definition an attainable goal only for the very, very few. For you and me, the majority, to compare ourselves with them, to try and emulate them, is simply to court failure against far too ambitious a target.

Take up your 20% of slack, however, and really settle into your new, much improved level of performance and something wonderful happens. Another twenty becomes possible, so that over a reasonable period of time that goal of excellence really does come within reach. There is another benefit. This steady ratcheting up of improvements seems acceptable and unthreatening to others, whereas the wide-eyed new convert to the idol of excellence only attracts resentment, ridicule and opposition.

There are a variety of 20%s to be claimed in an organisational sense. Better credit control and cash flow management; better materials handling; improved quality control and distribution, and so on.

*You* however are the easiest target of all – in your personal life and in terms of contribution to your organisation, be it office, factory or home. Know yourself, what you want and what others want from you, and you can package yourself, your product or organisation far more effectively.

There are strong parallels in the way we talk about people, products and organisations. We talk about an individual's personality, about brand personalities and about corporate personalities. We talk about dress sense, about product packaging, about architecture and about corporate design. By using a mix of successful techniques from the social skills and from brand and corporate management, remarkable results can be achieved. We can package and market *ourselves* better, and in turn give our products and companies the kind of human characteristics which research tells us will lead to success.

This is not a traditional self-improvement handbook, many of which can already be found on the bookshelves. It is altogether more ambitious than that.

Instead it aims to expose and help you change damaging attitudes and images, and to help you create a far better climate in which you, your product and your organisation can prosper.

First impressions and presentation are vital and *The 20% Factor* gives the blunt, sometimes barely palatable advice you need to put your very best face forward.

*Graham Lancaster*
*March 1993*

# HOW TO USE THE 20% FACTOR

There is a great deal of truth in the old fable of the tortoise and the hare. None of us wants to be thought of as a plodder, but the fact is that for most people, the best way to get on is by achieving steady unspectacular improvements. In this way the grey suited 'tortoise' will often overtake the showy, flash-in-the pan management 'hare'.

This book will show how easy it is to improve your performance in many key areas by 20%. 20% is a worthwhile achievement in itself. But what is really exciting is the knowledge that you can go on improving by another 20% after a while, and then another, and another. In fact if you improve by 20% four times over a period, then you will have increased your performance potential by over *100 per cent* on your original base. Do that and very few flashy hares will pass you again.

The structure of the book is in four main parts:

**Part One** is Know You Can Improve by 20%. This gives you a base from which to measure your progress. Self-completion tests also help you understand your broad character traits as others may see them, and train you to be aware of pitfalls.

**Part Two** is A 20% Better You. This gives practical tips on how to make a better first impression.

**Part Three** is A 20% Better Manager. Once you have begun to present yourself better as an individual, this part gives tips on how to use this new knowledge to improve your effectiveness as a manager.

**Part Four** – Win with the 20% Factor – is designed for regular on-going use over the coming months and years to help you to keep up a continuous programme of 20% Factor improvements.

# KNOW YOU CAN IMPROVE BY

# 20%

The difference between success and failure is often a very small margin.

In Part 1 you are encouraged to think about yourself, and how others see you, clinically and objectively.

# 1 KNOW YOURSELF

### KNOW YOURSELF

Socrates, the Greek philosopher, was born in Athens around 470 BC. He left no written works for schoolchildren to hate to learn, and so learn to hate. Let young Plato get all the blame. He did however develop the Delphic theme of 'know thyself' – perhaps the best advice ever given.

Good advice is not always welcome of course. Socrates went about unfashionably promoting moral virtue, and they poisoned him for it. Beware of Greeks bearing grudges. Knowing yourself, however, is the first step in *The 20% Factor*.

You don't have to change very much about yourself to achieve substantial improvements in your management skills. A small improvement of, say, five per cent can improve your success rate by 20% or more. Not much when you consider we use less than 15 per cent of our reasoning power throughout our lives.

The difference between success and failure is often a very small margin. Less than a heartbeat may separate Olympic sprinters in a 100 metre final, but there is only one winner – ahead by a hundredth of a second. A tiny advantage in the engine, chassis or tyres of a racing car can result in a string of chequered flags.

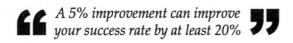

> **❝** *A 5% improvement can improve your success rate by at least 20%* **❞**

It's the same for you and me. You know the feeling when you have just missed a train you really needed to catch. Standing at the barrier, watching it leave, you start the 'if only' game. If only there had not been roadworks on the way to the station. If only it had not been your turn to take the children to school. If only all the traffic lights had been green instead of red. But is it the train's fault it left on time? No. It was yours for not giving yourself a better margin of chance in which to catch it. You just missed the train. The train didn't miss you.

It's exactly the same in business. Very often a small margin distinguishes the successful people who are offered jobs and promotions; a small margin usually separates companies who are market leaders from the followers. As Tom Peters said in *A Passion For Excellence*, 'Advantage comes not from the spectacular or the technical. Advance comes from a persistent seeking of the mundane edge'.

> **""** *Remember the fable of the tortoise and the hare – 20% steady improvements are better than a 100% leap in the dark* **""**

So do the wise thing. Improve yourself by a succession of small, achievable margins. *The 20% Factor*. You'll be surprised how often that small margin is enough to make you the winner.

> **""** *A daunting 100% is five gulps of an easy-to-swallow 20%* **""**

## IF YOU CAN'T MEASURE IT YOU CAN'T MANAGE IT

To improve, you have to have a base line against which to measure progress. If you can't measure things, you can't manage them.

The first – and toughest – task is to get to know yourself. *Really* know yourself. Your strengths and weaknesses. None of us can ever be really objective about ourselves, but the specially devised self-analysis tests in this book will help.

## FIRST IMPRESSIONS

Four or five seconds. That's how long it takes for important people to form an opinion of you on first meeting. This is not merely a first impression – although it is that as well – it is their *entire* opinion. Anything you do or say after these first few seconds may strengthen this opinion. Or begin the long and notoriously difficult job of changing it – because none of us likes to change our judgements.

Research shows how important non-rational and emotional factors are in this complex process – often outweighing rational assessment. For example, Michael Argyle of Oxford University has estimated that non-verbal cues have 4.3 times the effect of verbal cues.

Theodore Levitt, the management expert, says 'commonsense tells us and research confirms that people use appearance to make judgements about reality'.

> **""** *A 20% increase in non-verbal cues is the equivalent of saying over 80% more* **""**

You are what you seem. You will be pigeon-holed, labelled in fairly indelible ink and filed accordingly. And it is this gap between how influential people see us, and how we want to be seen, that is at the heart of so much unhappiness, poor morale and disappointment. Because first impressions last.

## DIY ANALYSIS

I would now like you to begin completing the first of our self-analysis assessments to help you know yourself. I think you will find them fun to work on – but do give your responses seriously. Don't try and double guess what you think might be the 'good' or 'correct' answers. There are no right and wrong answers. Only *your* answers – and that's what we need if you are to achieve the first goal of really knowing yourself.

Many organisations use personality and psychometric testing to evaluate candidates for jobs and to appraise their existing people. These can indicate your degree of introversion/extraversion, or your NPF (a neurotic personality factor to measure your emotional stability and stress tolerance), your general intelligence and non-verbal intelligence quotients (IQ) or your response patterns to other people. Even where formal tests are not given, experienced interviewers use their finely honed antennae to form their own judgements on these factors based on experience they have obtained empirically over many years.

The self-completion exercises which follow are designed to train you to think about yourself and your responses. Do not take the results too literally, simply enjoy the exercises and remember that others will be forming opinions of you in similar ways.

If you want a detailed professional analysis of your personality and aptitudes use an agency which meets the Codes of Practice and ethical standards of the British Psychological Society.

---

## ASSESS YOUR PERSONALITY - EXERCISE

1. Pick the shape below which best represents your personality. Don't think about it. Your first response is most revealing.

2. Which of these shapes do you find most appealing? Pick one from each group and circle the letter of your choice.

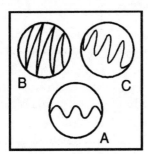 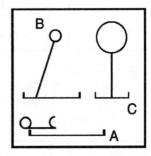

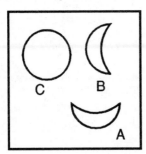 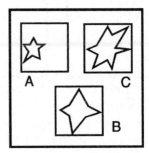

3. If you were asked to draw a tree which of these would it most resemble?

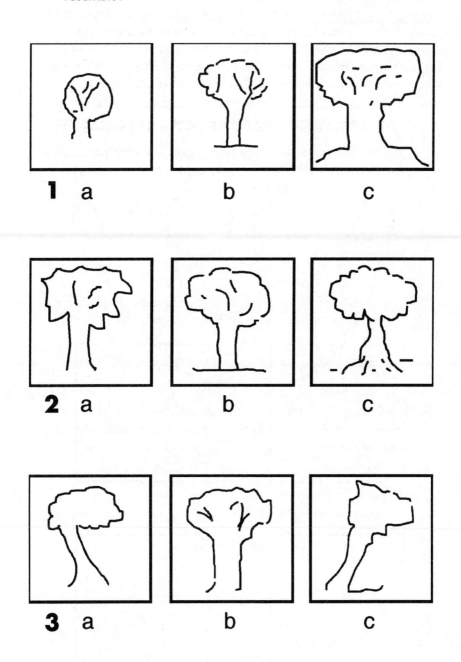

**1** a        b        c

**2** a        b        c

**3** a        b        c

4.  Glance quickly at the picture below. Is the face

    *a smiling*  or
    *b scowling?*

5.  Hold a pencil at arm's length and, with both eyes open, line it up with a straight edge such as a door or window frame. Close each eye in turn. Did the pencil move furthest with your

    *a right eye closed*
    *b left eye closed?*

6.  Imagine you are sighting a rifle or looking through a telescope. Would you close your

    *a right eye*  or
    *b left eye?*

7.  Clasp your hands comfortably in your lap. Is your

    *a left*  or
    *b right thumb on top?*

8. What is your normal writing position? Does the nib point

   *a upwards on the paper* or
   *b down the paper with your hand covering the tip?*

9. Sign your name in the space below. Now compare it with the sample below. Is your signature:

   *a Larger*
   *b Smaller*
   *c About the same size?*

*MArtn Smithson*

10. Do you usually sign your name as:

   *a Name plus one initial only? (eg D Smith)*
   *b Name plus two initials? (eg D L Smith)*
   *c First and second name? (eg Donald Smith)*
   *d All your names? (eg Donald Leslie Smith)*

11. Do you underline your signature as in the illustration below?

   *a Always*
   *b Occasionally*
   *c Seldom or never*

*Rdan Jevmul*

12. Connect the dots by drawing a continuous line through each in turn, starting at 1 and ending at 36. Use a fairly long (about 6") pencil and hold it at the furthest end from the point. Take as much time as you like.

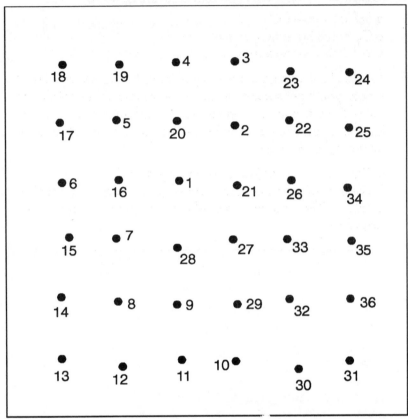

13. Make a cross in each box, using first your left and then your right hand, keeping the arm as straight as possible.

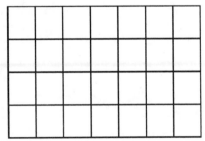

14. You have been given three hot racing tips. The first two romp home, bringing you £600. Chancing it all on the third horse could mean winning £2000 or losing the lot. Do you:

    *a Bet the whole lot?*
    *b Go home happily with your winners*
    *c Risk half your winnings on the third horse?*

15. It looks like it's going to rain as you leave the house for work. If it does you'll get soaked because you've lots of business to do out of the office today. On the other hand if the sun shines the last thing you want is to be burdened with a raincoat, or even an umbrella. So will you:

    *a Carry an umbrella just to be on the safe side*
    *b Wear a raincoat because it would be wretched to get soaked*
    *c Take neither coat nor umbrella in the optimistic hope that it stays fine?*

## RESULTS AND ANALYSIS

### 1. What your choice of symbol reveals

### Triangle
The only symbol with a clear sense of direction, the triangle is like an arrowhead speeding through space.

You are more ambitious than most, setting clear targets in life and working towards them with single minded dedication. A natural leader, you are also likely to be something of a workaholic, perhaps sacrificing family life and friendships in your eagerness to achieve your goals.

*Your ideal career.* Any job offering power as well as responsibility, where your efforts will be rewarded by prompt recognition and rapid promotion.

### Square
The most logical symbol, with four right angles, the square is chosen by equally logical people.

You prefer facts and figures, rather than guesswork, when solving problems or reaching decisions. Your dislike of hunches and distrust of intuition means you assess challenging situations objectively rather than emotionally.

*Your ideal career.* A job where you are able to work with facts rather than feelings, such as banking, accountancy, law, science or technology.

### Squiggle
The most eccentric of the four symbols, this is the first choice of people who take a rather off-beat view of life.

You have boundless enthusiasm and energy coupled with a need to become involved in a wide range of activities. You hate routine, loathe being pinned down and are at your best when able to enjoy plenty of variety.

*Your ideal career.* Working in television, newspapers, advertising, public relations or any job involving a fast-paced lifestyle.

### Circle
The circle, found in many religions, is the most harmonious of the four symbols.

You are skilled at dealing with other people, your warmth and understanding putting them quickly at ease. An empathic and sensitive person, you know intuitively how others feel and have the ability to respond in the most appropriate way.

*Your ideal career:* Any job where you deal with people rather than things: teaching, nursing, therapy, personnel management or selling.

## 2. Total the number of a, b and c shapes ticked.

If you scored mostly a's you'll prefer a quiet life and find pleasure in solitude. You would sooner stay at home listening to the radio than go out to parties, and enjoy intimate dinners for two rather than dining out with lots of friends. A somewhat diffident person, you shun the limelight and would far rather work behind the scenes.

If you scored mostly b's you are highly sociable, need constant variety and actively seek out lively surroundings. An impulsive person, you'd far sooner do something on the spur of the moment than plan every detail carefully. A lively party gives you far more enjoyment than staying home.

You adore being the centre of attention and feel depressed if unable to command centre stage. Also you dislike solitude and love the company of those who are as lively and sociable as yourself.

If you scored mainly c's you enjoy being sociable but feel equally content with quieter activities, either alone or with a close companion. You are not worried by periods of solitude provided these don't last too long. You appreciate a certain amount of change and variety, but again feel stressed if denied periods of calm in which to recuperate.

Where scores are very close, you are able to change from one type of behaviour to the next, becoming outgoing or retiring as the situation demands.

## 3. Trees
### How big is your tree – small, medium or large?
The more space your tree drawing occupies the greater your self-confidence. If your tree looks small (see 1a) you lack confidence and are probably rather too shy for your own good. If it is closer to 1b you have high self-esteem and are reasonably self-assured. A tree occupying as much space as 1c reveals tremendous confidence and high self-esteem. You are simply bursting with energy and enthusiasm.

### Is the base of your tree filled in or open?
Absence of roots (2a) betrays a certain insecurity. You lack faith in yourself. A partly filled base (2b) suggests you have a stronger sense

of self, while a drawing with roots and surrounding ground details (2c) indicates a very strong sense of self.

## Does your tree lean to right or left?

If your tree leans left (3a) it reveals a desire to cling to the past and a reluctance to face the future. An upright tree (3b) means you are present-orientated, living very much for the moment. A right leaning tree (3c) shows a yearning to escape from an unsatisfactory present into a more desirable and rewarding future.

**Questions 4–8**. Total your scores

**4.** a 1   b 4
**5.** a 1   b 4
**6.** a 1   b 4
**7.** a 4   b 1
**8.** a 1   b 4

## Score 17–20

You would sooner rely on intuition than logic when solving problems. Artistic, creative and imaginative, you often find yourself drifting away into a private fantasy world. Impulsive and spontaneous, you are sensitive to other's emotions you can assess them accurately on first meeting. Look for a job where you can work with people rather than things and use your powers of imagination to the full.

## 11–14

You can be either logical or intuitive as the occasion demands. This enables you to be equally at home when using your creative powers or reasoning out solutions to difficult problems. You can demonstrate emotions but usually are able to control your feelings and deal with the situation using reason and objectivity.

Find a job which allows you to work with facts and figures but which also involves dealing with other people a good part of the time.

## 5–8

You find answers more by logic than intuition. When making decisions or solving problems you analyse objectively the facts and distrust those who jump to conclusions.

Careful and methodical, you dislike emotional scenes and get annoyed when people behave irrationally.

Look for a job where you can handle facts and figures rather than dealing with human emotions.

**9.**

**a** You have a strong sense of self-worth and high esteem. Self-confident and assertive, you'd sooner lead than be led. You enjoy being the centre of attention. The larger your signature the more this will hold true.

**b** You tend to be a rather shy, retiring person who shuns the limelight, preferring instead to work behind the scenes. You are sensitive to the feelings of others. The smaller your signature the more this will hold true.

**c** You are a fairly assertive person who can stand up for yourself most of the time, but may have difficulty dealing with overly dominant individuals.

**10.**

**a** and **b** Your motto might be moderation in all things. You are a careful, cautious, conscientious person who dislikes change and prefers convention to the unconventional, the familiar to the novel. You would sooner have a job involving routine and security than one which offers constant variety and change.

**c** and **d** You seek change for its own sake, enjoy meeting people and finding fresh activities. You tend to be something of a rebel, rejecting establishment views. You love the novel and unusual, in arts, drama and fashion. An idealist, you may sometimes lack a sufficiently practical approach to life.

**11.** If your signature is always underlined (a), you are very self-confident and enthusiastic. Occasional underlining (b) suggests occasional bouts of confidence and enthusiasm.

## Questions 12–13.
Total your scores

**12.** Score 12 if you managed to draw through *all* the dots; 8 if you missed up to six dots or made an incorrect change of direction and score 4 if you missed more than six dots.

**13.** Score 12 if you never crossed a line when making the cross; 8 if you crossed up to six lines and 4 if more than six lines were crossed.
   Now add both the scores together to discover how well coordinated

you are. But remember, this test is dependent on age and any physical disability.

## 20–24
You are extremely well coordinated physically and should excel at sports requiring accurate hand eye movements.

## 12–16
You have average physical coordination. This is a good score for anybody aged 35 and over. If you are in your early twenties and physically fit, it should be possible to improve physical balance through a sport which trains hand-eye coordination, such as tennis, squash, golf, archery or shooting.

## 8
You do not appear to be very well physically coordinated. Why not take the test again, since anxiety could have adversely influenced your score. And remember these tests are only intended as a general guide. It could be that you are extremely skilled at some activities requiring good hand/eye coordination, such as playing darts or climbing ladders.

## Questions 14 and 15.
Add together your scores on these questions

**14.** *a* 6   *b* 4   *c* 2
**15.** *a* 2   *b* 4   *c* 6

## Total score 10–12
You go for broke when taking a risky decision, always expecting a favourable outcome. You tend to believe luck plays a big part in success, and take the optimistic view that if something can go right for you it will do so. This means you can win big – but lose big too!

## 6–8
You like to hedge your bets to avoid having regrets over a missed opportunity. A somewhat cautious person, you are prepared to take a chance on occasions, but fear of making a big loss causes you to avoid high risks.

## 4
You hate the thought of losing and seek to minimise the feelings of anxiety, guilt and regret which come from sustaining even a modest loss. While you are seldom tempted to lose big by taking needless risks, this approach also leads you to miss many good opportunities.

**"** *20% of an average working month is 32 hours. Devote this much time to improving yourself – that's just 1 hour a day* **"**

## WHAT'S YOUR IQ?

When assessing your personality it is also useful to know your intelligence quotient (IQ). IQ tests are commonly used to assess suitability for jobs and promotions.

Traditionally IQ testing has been important amongst children, given its relevance to educational and schools issues in society. A definition of IQ is the ratio between a child's mental age (MA) and his or her chronological age (CA).

$$IQ = \frac{MA}{CA} \times 100$$

The mental age reflects the ability of a person to perform certain functions, plotted against the average performance of the population over an age range of 15–16 year olds. For example, if a person of 20 performs the same in the standard IQ tests as an average ten year old, his or her MA is ten. The person's chronological age, of course, is twenty. This would give a low IQ rating of 50:

$$\left( \frac{10}{20} \times 100 \right)$$

For adults, however, calculating IQ using this formula rapidly becomes misleading.

The average person reaches adult mental age when between 15 and 16 years of age. It tends to stay the same until around 25–30, after which a very gradual decline sets in. The average IQ range for 50 per cent of the population is between 90 and 110. By the age of seventy, however, the average man would have an IQ of around 80.[*] A good IQ test will feature a large number of items to iron out chance elements. An adult test will give the average person a score of 100, based on a good spread of people. A person's individual score is compared with the average – dividing his or her score by the average and multiplying by 100. Only some 0.5 per cent of adults have IQs of 140 or over.

---

[*]D Wechsler, *Intelligence Changes with Age*, Public Health Report, USA. 1942, supplement no. 168.

A good general mental ability test is the MD5, a 57 item paper/pencil test published by The Test Agency in High Wycombe. If you plan to have an IQ test or professional psychological test, ensure that you use an agency with methods and qualifications recognised by the British Psychological Society.*

---

### INTELLIGENT OR STREET WISE?

When I interview people I look for evidence of 'intelligence' – by which I really mean brightness and quickness of mind, rather than the much more scientific intelligence measurements I'm referring to here. As an employer you can give people experience, training and all kinds of help to mould them to your needs. But the one thing you can't give somebody is 'intelligence'.

Let me give you an inside tip, however. If someone presents themselves to me well – in the ways I'm going to describe later – if they make me like them, if they seem to reflect my own views and values, if I think they like me ... then I bet I credit them with being bright and intelligent. Because they are like me, and all of us think we're intelligent, don't we?

Call it being street wise, but you can get people to credit you with a higher IQ than you may possess by using this technique.

---

## YOUR IQ RATING – HELP OR HINDRANCE?

Don't boast! Don't panic! You are likely to be average. But if you are below average on IQ testing don't panic. And if you are above average, don't start boasting about joining MENSA and becoming a chess grandmaster! The reality is that intelligence and brains have a lot less to do with business success than you think. And in any case 80 per cent of your intelligence is inherited.

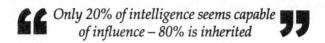

**“** *Only 20% of intelligence seems capable of influence – 80% is inherited* **”**

A survey commissioned by a firm of recruitment specialists (Robert Half) showed that only 1 per cent of senior managers put

---

*The British Psychological Society (48 Princess Road East, Leicester LE1 7DR) operates a Certification Scheme to maintain high standards of psychological and occupational testing.

'intelligence' as the key reason for business success. Top of their list (56 per cent) was 'sheer determination', followed by 'hard work' (13.7 per cent).

---

### KNOWING LEFT FROM RIGHT

The interplay between the left and right hemispheres of our brain contributes significantly to the way we behave. For right-handed people the left hemisphere is thought to be where the learning process takes place, where information, facts and experiences are taken in and sorted logically. It also controls speech. The right deals more with senses and feelings – our non-verbal side, so important in developing winning human and business relationships.

In his book *The Separated Hemispheres*, Roger W Sperry suggests that educational systems, as well as science in general, have tended to neglect this important right hemisphere non-verbal form of intellect.

---

Robert Townsend, author of *Up the Organisation*, suggested in an address to the Industrial Society that managers in any case use only some 20% of their intellect at work.

IQ testing is now seen as only one of many yardsticks used by employers. In any case it can throw up some real anomalies. For example, two people doing the same type of job, one with a high IQ and one a low IQ, could each have a reputation for being lazy underachievers. However, one could be so bored and un-stretched as to achieve low performance levels, the other because the job was too tough for him to meet his targets.

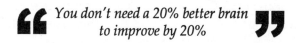
> ❝ *You don't need a 20% better brain to improve by 20%* ❞

Employers know from examples like this that IQ can influence levels of job satisfaction and labour turnover. And it is not unusual for a hard working, reliable person of average intelligence (and consequently with a much higher boredom threshold) to be preferred for promotion to someone much brighter. So, while *The 20% Factor* may not be able to improve your IQ, be reassured that you don't have to be 'brainy' to be successful. Elbow grease is every bit as important as eminence grise and Hercule Poirot's 'little grey cells'.

## PART 1 CHECKLIST

- A 5% improvement can improve your success rate by 20% or more
- First impressions last
- Improve yourself by a succession of small, achieveable margins
- What people see is four times more effective than what they hear
- It takes hard work and determination – not just brains – to succeed!

# PART 2

# A

# 20%

# BETTER YOU

Part 1 was designed to encourage self-assessment, and to appreciate that others form their opinions of you in fairly predictable ways. It can be a shock to realise that the complex physiology that is *you* – the unique cocktail of flesh, bones, blood and soul which makes you an individual – is pigeon-holed so superficially and so quickly by people who matter.

Once you realise this, however, and have a fair idea of how you currently come across, you can cease to be passive. Using *The 20% Factor* you can go on the offensive and shape how people see and respond to you.

Part 2, then, is a guide to how *The 20% Factor* can create a better you by looking at how you can make the most of your physical appearance, dress sense, background, sex and interpersonal skills.

# 2  FACIAL PREJUDICE

There is not much that we can do about our face. It is, however, likely to have a major influence on our chances of success.

In his book *Contact: The First Four Minutes*, written with Natalie Zunin, psychiatrist Leonard Zunin suggests that four minutes is how long it takes people to decide whether or not to develop relationships (Ballantine Books, New York, 1972). The face has a lot to do with this. Any barrister will tell you that juries can be heavily influenced by how a defendant looks and presents his or herself. Having a 'criminal's face' means you are more likely to be treated like a criminal and to act like one. The State of Texas even used to spend a proportion of its budget for rehabilitating offenders on plastic surgery as a reward for good behaviour. (Now it is directed at the most needy.)

---

### THE JURY'S OUT

In the USA there has been extensive research into the impact on juries of the way a defendant looks and presents him or herself. Harry Kalven and Hans Zeisel have done much pioneering work in this area. One case reported concerned a man charged with raping his daughter, aged ten. He was found guilty and given a life sentence. On appeal the jury came up with a hung verdict at the re-trial. Then, at the third trial, the jury declared a not guilty verdict, and even gave the man 68 dollars they had chipped in to show their sympathy.

Presumably, come trial three with different jurors, the man's ability to project himself and his side of the story had improved dramatically. That was some time ago, but the advent of video technology has given lawyers the opportunity to coach clients and even witnesses.

---

These are murky waters. There was a time when 'science' was applied to the study of the face. Jonathan Kaspar Lavater, a Swiss, developed techniques which he claimed could predict a person's personality from their face, based on such measurements as the size of nose and distance between the eyes. Charles Darwin's eccentric cousin, Sir Francis Galton (a pioneer of fingerprinting) launched his own system for the 'measurement' of attractiveness, and promoted selective mating – a 'science' he called *eugenics*. Craniology, the science which deals with variations in size, shape and proportions of skulls among different races, had also been developed, paving the way for untold quasi-scientific racism. Sweden's Anders Retzius developed a cranial index classifying head shapes, which led to endless debate about skull size, the size of brain and level of intelligence. The shape of things to come arrived in the form of the Italian Cesare Lombroso, who came up with a link between a receding forehead and the propensity to commit crime. In 1876 he published '*L'uomo delinquente*' (The Delinquent Man), arguing that criminals are born, not made, and have identifiable characteristics.

## JEKYLL AND HYDE

Literature is peppered with such stuff and it has left its influence on us today – Shakespeare's *Shylock*, Dickens' *Fagin*, Hugo's *Quasimodo*. One book that really captures the intangibility of physical appearance and our intuitive, physiognomical reaction to it is Robert Louis Stevenson's *The Strange Case of Dr Jekyll and Mr Hyde*. Mr Hyde is described as giving an impression of deformity without any nameable malformation, he had a displeasing smile ... all these points were against him; but not all of these together could explain the hitherto unknown disgust, loathing and fear with which Mr Utterson regarded him. "There must be something else," said the perplexed gentleman. "There *is* something more ... Or can it be the old story of Dr Fell?"'

Stevenson was referring to a verse by Thomas Brown dating to the seventeenth century:

*I do not love you, Dr Fell,*
*But why I cannot tell;*
*But this I know full well,*
*I do not love you, Dr Fell.*

It captures that feeling we sometimes have about people (and they may have about us!) – we don't like the look of them, but we can't quite put our finger on exactly *why*.

BEETHOVEN'S DEATH MASK

Even Beethoven did not escape some of this type of questionable science of the face. When in 1827 he died in Vienna, the doctors conducted a post-mortem to discover, amongst other things, why his brain was so musical. His death mask was made after the post-mortem, and is less accurate as a result.

## FACE UP AND TAKE ACTION!

To stack the odds most strongly in your favour you should aim to look average, ordinary. Psychologist Les Posen says, 'From an early age we try to make sense of the world or to make it conform to what we want it to be – a safe, predictable place'. We categorise our world crudely into 'in' groups and 'out' groups. All the research shows that we like average, pleasant people – 'people like us', people who don't threaten us. The thing to remember is that *ordinariness is a key component of attractiveness* and that it is the absence of contrived distinguishing features that leads to that ordinariness/attractiveness.

It can be a mistake for those who are naturally very attractive to look too stunning. This can threaten others important to your success. Apart from envy, highly attractive people are sometimes thought empty headed, trivial and shallow. Take a lesson from nature and merge with your surroundings. Charles Darwin called it *cryptic coloration*, and it works.

## COSMETIC COVER-UP

In Japan – where 'face' has two meanings – there has been a near epidemic amongst university students undergoing plastic surgery to improve their chances of employment. Plastic and general cosmetic surgery is common enough in the West too, especially in those professions like acting, modelling and the media where facial blips seem unacceptable. That hollow-cheeked, pouty beauty of some models is created by the removal of the sixes, sevens and eights teeth, which partially collapses the cheeks. Capping teeth is also common and highly effective.

## MATURITY

People in their early to mid-twenties are generally greatly concerned about maturity – will employers or buyers see them as young and therefore inexperienced?

Amongst graduates I have generally found women a good three or four years ahead of men in terms of apparent maturity. Men still have a lot of prejudice working for them in other respects, so young women should play the maturity card for all its worth.

At the other extreme, men of mature years do seem to try too hard to seem younger – more so than women. A sentence or two from one of the short stories of Truman Capote's *Music for Chameleons* (Hamish Hamilton, London, 1982) captures this beautifully. His character, suddenly feeling old at fifty two, describes the old days when women found him attractive: 'I always had such confidence. Just walking down the street, I felt such a *swing*. I could feel people looking at me – on the street, in a restaurant, at a party' .... Now he seems to have become the invisible man and the pretty women at a recent party just saw him as 'a tired old guy who smiled too much'.

If you believe you have a serious facial problem affecting you psychologically, then talk to your doctor and decide if cosmetic surgery is possible and sensible. My own feeling is that cosmetic surgery should *not* be undertaken unless your medical adviser believes you are facing strong psychological problems in connection with your appearance. None of us is perfect, or perfectly ordinary. The main point I want to make is that it is those aspects of how you *choose* to present yourself that matter most. These are what give others clues to the type of person you may be. Most people realise that physical features such as height, prominent chins, birth marks etc are not within a person's control, and so will not jump to conclusions based on these physical characteristics. As an example of this, we all know how very quickly we forget about a stranger's serious disability once their personality becomes known to us. There are however cosmetic *choices* we make or ignore in connection with our appearance. These can have an irrational importance to others.

## QUIFFS AND NIFFS

■ Keep hair short, tidy – and strictly on your head!

■ The cut of your hair – for men and women – can help broaden or lengthen your face.

■ Certain hair styles will communicate very specific messages. In men, hair that is too long or cut aggressively short, in terms of the prevailing fashion, will be inviting comment. Although fashions and styles change, the principle of cryptic coloration still holds good. At any point in time there will be hair styles which are making a statement to the outside world – be it an arresting geometric cut, pre-Raphaelite organised chaos or bottle blond. For most business situations that kind of style may send signals to the people who matter which have more to do with your hairdresser's taste and persuasive skills than your own judgement. You know what is an average-looking hair style and cut for you and your age: stick to that.

■ Don't touch up greying hair, or wear toupees or hair pieces. There is a fair to good chance your helping hand to nature will be noticed, and all manner of meanings read into it – ranging from vanity to signs of downright dishonesty.

■ Avoid facial hair, unless you have a really noticeable scar, birth mark, 'weak' mouth or chin and neck problem to disguise.

■ Many employers are distrustful of beards and moustaches, and associate them with having something to hide, or as having Castro-like anarchical tendencies. This applies particularly in private industry, although in some fields – education, research, the arts – it may matter less, if at all. It is noticeable, however, that most public figures with beards from the world of business are self-made men – that small minority of people who can make their own rules. But even they have customers, and risk pogonophobia – the hatred of beards.

■ Men should minimise 'seven o'clock shadow'; if necessary by carrying a battery shaver in their briefcase. Swarthiness will be noticed. Politicians and others who may be called upon to appear on television at short notice have been known to carry their own powder puff to disguise the shadow beard!

■ If you suffer from hair in your nostrils and ears, ask your barber to attend to it for you. Small physical idiosyncrasies like this can have surprisingly major effects on how people react to you.

■ Bad breath and body odour have been the subject of any number of amusing TV commercials and bar-room jokes. But a joke it is not. Serious and persistent bad breath merits a discussion with your doctor. Twice a day tooth brushing, flossing, a mouth wash and a pocketful of peppermints, however, will take care of most problems. Naturally, injudicious enjoyment of garlic, curry, spring onions or alcohol will tell your boss or customer more about your judgement than about your taste in cuisine and wines.

---

### SPLITTING HAIRS

There was a marvellous parliamentary exchange in the House of Commons between the then Labour Prime Minister Harold Wilson, and the late Sir Gerald Nabarro, a flamboyant Tory MP with a huge moustache. Wilson was speaking in a defence debate about the trichotomy of demands on the budget – from the army, navy and air force – when Nabarro shot up and said the word should be pronounced as *tri* not *try*-chotomy. Quick as a flash Wilson insisted his own pronunciation was perfectly correct, and perhaps the Honourable Member had confused it with the word trichology – the study of unwanted facial hair, at last a subject on which the Honourable Member had some knowledge. The House exploded with laughter.

---

## WARPAINT

Women have far more decisions to make about their facial appearance.

It is impossible to generalise about makeup, except to say that wearing none at all might seem as odd to an employer as your wearing either 'too much', or colours at the very leading edge of fashion. The message here is *play safe*. Look attractive, but not threateningly so. Soft, muted colours are always safest; grey-browns for eyes and warm apricot-peaches for lips/cheeks work well for all colour types. Double guess how you think people important to you want you to appear, and within sensible limits be the type of person they want.

Is it really that important? Yes! As an example, research by Dr Walter Berger (with Heinz Schuler) of the University of Ausburg, Germany, showed how eighty personnel managers reacted to faked job application forms, each with a photograph attached. The results proved that the more attractive applicants in the photographs stood a much better chance of being asked in for an interview, and that they were thought likely to be more friendly, more creative and more highly motivated than the rest.

## OTHER HELPFUL HINTS

■ Spectacles should again be ordinary and not worthy of remark. If they are too fashionable, too expensive looking, or equally too starkly utilitarian, beware. Unless you need them medically, avoid tinted lenses – they can make you look shifty or threatening. If necessary, purchase some contact or light reactive photochromic lenses.

■ Handshakes are important. They should be dry and firm and accompanied by both eye contact and a smile in most situations. Bonecrushing handshakes should not be used. Unfortunately some people perspire when nervous and this can lead to sweaty palms. The only answer is a quick but thorough wipe dry on your side clothing before shaking hands.

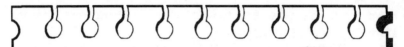

## SUMMARY

You can't improve your inherited facial characteristics unless you resort to drastic action – but
you *can* apply *The 20% Factor* to improve the
image you project:

- Play safe – aim to look average
- Make the most of your assets
- Don't fix your face – project your personality
- Smile – and feel 20% better!

# 3 GET SMART!

The best advice I can give on dressing for business echoes the message to play safe, and merge with your surroundings. In general terms, your choice of dress should reflect your organisation's values, not your own. If you are unsure about whether to wear certain clothes to the office – don't. Dress as a television newscaster might – appear timeless, classless and unobtrusive.

Men should wear the following:

- Dark blue or grey suits, plain or pin-striped (not brown or tweed)
- White, pale blue or striped shirts
- Muted tie
- Little if any male jewellery.

Avoid the following:

- Blazers, sports jackets, or sweaters or cardigans in winter.
- Conspicuous designer labels (and if you are in junior to middle management, do not outdress your superiors).

■ Keep the Cartier tank watch or gold Rolex Oyster for the evenings – even if they are just Hong Kong fakes. Ordinary people do not wear them.

■ Iron out any other idiosyncrasies in your dress choice – the pocket handkerchief, the button-hole rose, the bow tie, the hat, the suede shoes, the tweed cape, the Gucci briefcase.

All the above just might strike a dischord for no apparent reason, and become a suspected clue to all kinds of peculiarities influential people may imagine you have.

**“** *Spend 20% more time and thought on your appearance* **”**

Others may also attach importance, surprisingly, to what may seem small or trivial matters. Specks of dandruff on your collar. Shoes not cleaned that morning, and in need of re-heeling. Trousers kneed and unpressed, and accordion sleeved jackets. That tiny, tiny spot of bolognese sauce on your favourite tie and which you feel sure no one will notice. A little too much after-shave. Finger nails that are too long, bitten to the quick or dirty.

Play safe. The key to creating a good impression is to aim for safe ordinariness. Headhunter John McManus says that the three most memorable job candidates he saw one year wore bow ties. None got the job!

And Paul Keers, author of *The Gentleman's Wardrobe* says, 'One of the keys to conservatism in men's dress is that the subtext to an adherence to traditional professional dress codes is an adherence to other forms of professional behaviour.'

## BUSINESS DRESS FOR WOMEN

Business dressing for women is far more complex, being touched by mercurial fashion trends. The central theme of plain, simple and businesslike, however, remains the same. Winter and autumn wear is easier – suits, high necked blouses and shirts and other such 'sensible' clothes and accessories. Spring and summer wear can lead to more difficult decisions. Take note of these tips:

■ Brassières and business remain a prudent combination.

■ Only opt out of stockings/tights in the hottest of weather.

■ Don't dress too sexily, whatever the prevailing fashions. Nothing too low, figure hugging or too short.

■ Muted colours – maroons, navys, beiges, greys, pastels and so on – are 'safer' for the office than strong primary colours.

■ Use your eyes. Notice how other successful people dress in the organisation and copy – yes copy – them.

■ If you are short, executive dress counsellors will advise you to wear heels and fitted outfits, especially waisted. Businesslike trousers can also make legs look longer and are particularly flattering with a matching long-line jacket (NB Japanese fashion houses designing for the West produce good clothes for shorter people).

■ Taller women can wear most things and are best advised to carry themselves as if they were not tall at all. Avoid stooping, even when in the company of short men – it can be seen as patronising. Flat shoes and pumps obviously help.

---

### TRICKS FOR SMALLER WOMEN

■ DON'T choose big prints, chunky jewellery or large collars and cuffs – they can overwhelm small frames.

■ DO try long slim skirts and tapered trousers – they'll make your legs look longer.

■ DO think about tricks of the eye, like wearing vertical stripes. They always look smart and add length.

■ DO remember cropped jackets look good, as do all fitted styles.

■ DO go for clingy, stretchy, one-size Lycra. It's a good choice because it adapts well to all figures.

■ DON'T be tempted to add height by wearing high heels with everything. Choose shoe styles that are appropriate to the outfit.

■ DO break the fashion rules if you fall in love with some wild, boldly patterned, non-tailored outfit or a beautiful piece of jewellery. If it makes you feel great, then it's for you.

(Copyright of *Good Housekeeping* magazine and used with permission.)

■ Fashion experts advise larger women to emphasise your good points as much as cover up what you feel are the bad. Draw attention to an attractive neck, hands and arms, shapely legs, bustline and so on.

---

### TRICKS FOR LARGER WOMEN

■ DO emphasise your good points as much as covering up the bad. Draw attention to shapely legs or a good neck and bustline.

■ DON'T buy a smaller size in the hope you'll slim into it. A size 22 does not flatter a size 24, it simply emphasises bulges, making it obvious that you are uneasy with your size.

■ DO choose colours that suit you, rather than always going for the 'slimming' darker colours.

■ DON'T settle for anything just because it fits: 'Too many women buy something they're not really happy with,' says Audrey Winkler, 'when if they did a little more research, they could find something they felt really good in, and would wear far more often. It's definitely worth paying more for one good item rather than having two or three not-quite-right ones that you hardly ever wear.'

(Copyright of *Good Housekeeping* magazine and used with permission.)

---

I repeat – your dress should reflect the values of your company more than your own idiosyncrasies. Sublimate some of those pangs of self-expression!

## SELL YOURSELF!

In isolation it is easy to dismiss some aspects of this kind of advice as trivial, even humorous. However there are serious implications of getting your image, your first impressions, wrong. Research suggests that 55 per cent of the impact we make is based on appearance, 38 per cent on our presentation of ourselves in terms of confidence, voice quality and accent, and just 7 per cent on what we actually say.

Research by the Institute of Manpower Studies published in 1988 suggested that the majority of people conducting interviews for jobs had no training in interviewing and took a defensive, play safe approach. They were concerned primarily with avoiding selecting a *wrong* candidate, rather than choosing the *right* one. I believe this is frequently the case in other buyer/seller business

## TROUBLE MAKER

In his book *Human Engineering* (Jonathan Cape, 1970, London), Lord Robens talks about the textile genius Richard Arkwright. Born in Bolton in 1732, Arkwright – the thirteenth child of poor parents – gave up his job as a barber at the age of 35 to invent and perfect a spinning frame powered by water. He became the richest cotton spinner in England and died with the then huge fortune of half a million pounds.

But, says Robens, a modern industrial organisation probably could not digest a new Arkwright. If such a man were recruited as a workman he would quickly be picked out as a trouble-maker; if he joined as a management trainee he would be even more rapidly identified as someone who 'won't fit in'.

relationships. So present yourself as a safe choice. Make it easy for them to choose you. And remember, they are probably insecure in having to make the decision. Help them achieve a safe, comforting encounter with you.

I'm not saying that all of this is right or fair. But that's the way it is, and if you realise it and accept it you'll have a head start over those who insist on being stubbornly individualistic.

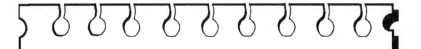

## SUMMARY

You don't need to spend 20% more to improve the way you dress, but remember to:

- Reflect the organisational culture
- Emulate successful superiors
- Create the best first impression
- Dress with skill, don't dress to kill!

# 4 HEALTH MATTERS

Looking – and ideally being – healthy is an important factor in popularity and acceptance. It is a factor which has significantly increased in importance over the last decade.

In part, this is a result of successful campaigns to encourage us to eat more healthily, cut out smoking, drink less alcohol and take more exercise. It is also due to greater public awareness of major illnesses and their consequences – particularly heart disease, cancer and HIV/AIDS.

## WINNING WEIGHS

Obesity is commonly defined as those 20% or more above normal weight for their height. For obese people their size is likely to be the first overall impression they will make on others.

Time was when corpulence in our leaders was thought to help bestow 'gravitas'. This is no longer the case, although big people can have a powerful and intimidating presence. Now, average weight is more likely to convey that impression of health and vitality others look for. Research shows that fat people are often seen as unbusinesslike and less intelligent than 'normal' sized individuals. They are assumed to be more prone to illness and some employers actively discriminate against them. Sloppy and disorganised are also accusations levelled at overweight people – 'if he or she can't organise themselves to stick to a diet, they are sure to be disorganised in other aspects of their life'.

*Obese people are defined as those 20% or more above normal weight for their height*

Insurance company tables are an indication of what we have been conditioned to think of as the normal parameters of size to weight. For example a 5 feet 9 inch man is expected to weigh between nine stone six pounds and fourteen stone six pounds: a five feet five inch woman between eight stone four pounds and twelve stone ten pounds.

There is no doubt that coming in at around average weight for your size (and as you can see that still leaves quite a margin) is going to help you create the best first impression.

Underweight people have less of an image problem, although those who are very thin can give the impression of bad health, weakness, lack of stamina and, again, a predisposition to regular illnesses. AIDS and anorexia can also suggest themselves, with all their accompanying, if unspoken, prejudices.

## SIZE UP THE SITUATION

It is interesting to recognise the great changes in what different generations regard as 'normal' size, because in the well-fed West we are all getting bigger every day.

On average, women are now two inches taller and a stone heavier than a hundred years ago. Eighteen inch waists were the height of fashion a century ago. For some this meant having two ribs removed, and for others deliberately acquiring a tape worm. If these forms of self-inflicted physical damage seem incredible to us now, is the self-induced anorexia or bulimia of today really any better?

Role models are getting tougher, however. In the last generation the average model weighed 8 per cent less than the average woman – today the difference is 23 per cent.

Even over the past 20 years there have been significant changes. The average woman today is five feet five inches in height, weighing nine stone nine point four pounds, measuring 36B–25½–36. This is almost half an inch taller than 20 years ago, and adds two inches to the bust. Retailers report that the most common bra size is now 36B: it was until quite recently 34B. Forty seven per cent of women are size 16 or larger, yet 45 per cent are under five feet four inches tall.

Men have shown parallel growth, as an examination of old military uniforms will demonstrate.

## GET FIGHTING FIT

Unlike size and weight, energy is not something that is easy to measure, although we soon recognise it when we see it in others. And we tend to find it almost invariably in those who take regular exercise – either in a health club, through running or playing a sport.

Exercise not only keeps weight under control, it builds muscle tone and, through encouraging better circulation, helps produce

---

### KEEPING FACE

I once heard a police chief advise any man who finds himself the subject of a random attack by a gang of high-spirited youths to sit on the floor and weep pathetically, offering neither resistance nor challenge. There is a fair chance, he thought, that they might treat you as beneath contempt, and not worth the loss of face involved in hitting you.

A northern England nightclub employs a dwarf as a bouncer – 'There's no glory in hitting a midget,' said the manager.

---

a clearer complexion and bright eyes. Although hyper-energy is not recommended, the impression of slothfulness should certainly be avoided.

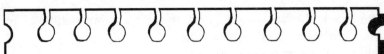

## SUMMARY

Good health helps, so get 20% fitter, not 20% fatter:

■ Watch your weight

■ Firm up flab!

■ Ooze energy.

# 5 BEATING THE BIGOTS

Just as you can't do much about your height or face, you can't do much about people typecasting you by nationality, religion, class, sex or sexual persuasion.

## PEOPLE PREJUDICE

There is nothing new in it of course. See how shocking the following 'descriptions' now seem to us. They are taken from *Beeton's Dictionary of Universal Information*, an early kind of household encyclopedia published around 120 years ago. Remember also that these entries would have been written by highly educated experts on their subject – not some bar-room bigot.

**Russians.** 'The manners of the people are, in general, far from cleanly. Drinking is a very common vice among them. Gambling is also prevalent. The Russian peasantry are in a very abject condition; and, morally speaking, the nobles are ignorant, proud, sensual and generally devoid of principle. The lower orders are equally coarse in their appetites, and, in many situations, equally open to charges of deceit and falsehood.'

**Irish.** 'That part of the inhabitants called the Wild Irish were formerly as savage as the native Americans and, like them, lived in huts, making a fire in the middle of them; but it is to be hoped that all the rude and barbarous customs, as well as every other trace of wretchedness and degradation, will vanish in time, and that a general industry will take the place of beggary ...'

**Chinese.** 'Their greatest and best good quality is a steady and unremitting industry. To balance this, however, they exhibit all the vices of mean and degraded minds. From the throne to the lowest subject, an utter and abhorrent disregard of truth prevails, and their unrivalled skill in every branch of the art of cheating, has been remarked, with astonishment, by all their mercantile visitors.'

**Egyptians.** 'The complexion of the Egyptians is tawny, and as we proceed southward they become darker, until those near Nubia are almost black. They are generally indolent and cowardly. The richer sort do nothing all day but drink coffee, smoke tobacco, and sleep, and they are ignorant, proud, haughty and ridiculously vain.'

**Persians** (Iranians). They get a better press – 'gay, lively and active. There is no country where the beard is regarded with such veneration, it being repeatedly during the day washed, combed and adjusted. They are the most learned people in the East ...' But even here there is a sting in the tail – 'morality is much studied in Persia, though little practised.'

**Portuguese.** You may have thought that our oldest ally would have fared well. Not so. 'The women in the capital are loose and dissolute; in the country the people are indolent and listless. A want of cleanliness is equally complained of in the capital and in the provincial towns.'

Have we changed much? A little. But I fear that national, racial and religious stereotypecasting remains a potent – if largely unspoken – force.

The significance of this, the economic dimension behind racial stereotypecasting, is more easily seen in the USA, where 1990 Census statistics are given with a racial breakdown. Figures published in 1992 showed that on average whites earned 59 per cent more than blacks, and 15 per cent less than Asians, who were generally better educated.

The best way to deal with prejudice is to follow the advice I have given about reflecting back a corporation's or boss's values, without losing whatever normal ethnic or religious dimension there is to your character. Unless you have been to Harrow or Eton, being more English than the English, or more Ivy League than the Ivy League is not advised. Nor is it a good idea to reflect back any racial prejudices you detect around you – Irish people telling Irish jokes against themselves, for example. I feel the same is true in connection with suspected homophobics or misogynists.

Few employers, however bigoted, will risk legal action under the various equality laws and codes, but prejudice is still a force. For all but the most extreme bigots, however, a willing, competent person who reflects with credit the organisation's values will be an attractive proposition, if only on the grounds of commercial self-interest. It is also true that most bigots have prejudices against *groups* of people, and tend to justify their bigotry in that way – not overtly against individuals who have that annoying habit of not fitting into the stereotype envisioned for the particular group.

## WHAT CLASS ARE YOU?

Another way in which we become pigeon-holed and stereotyped is through class. It is valuable to know how others will view you in this context.

The most widely used system for social grading is that agreed between Research Services Ltd and JICNARS, and is described in JICNARS' publication *Social Grading on the National Readership Survey*. See where you fit.

| SOCIAL GRADE | PERCENTAGE OF ALL ADULTS AGE 15+ | SOCIAL STATUS | OCCUPATION |
|---|---|---|---|
| A | 2.7 | Upper middle class | Higher managerial, administrative or professional |
| B | 15.1 | Middle class | Intermediate managerial, administrative or professional |
| C1 | 23.9 | Lower middle class | Supervisory or clerical, and junior managerial, administrative or professional |
| C2 | 27.8 | Skilled working class | Skilled manual workers |
| D | 17.8 | Working class | Semi and unskilled manual workers |
| E | 12.7 | Those at lowest level of subsistence | State pensioners or widows (no other earner), casual or lowest grade workers |

Britain, most of Europe and the US are far from meritocracies and class, in its various manifestations, will have an important effect on your business and social life. According to the Pareto principle, 20 per cent of people spend 80 per cent of the money. Know where you fit, and if you want to try and climb the social ladder understand some of the issues you will have to confront – ranging from snobbery to inverted snobbery.

**66** *20% of people spend 80% of the money* **99**
*– Pareto Principle*

## Unclassified social categories

Mixed class marriages face more difficulties than most and are more likely to end in divorce. This is exacerbated in those cases where a woman has married someone from a lower social group, when violence is more likely. A study in the US, reported by Dr Michael Argyle and Monika Henderson in their book *The Anatomy of Relationships* (William Heinemann, London, 1985) suggests that 45 per cent of husbands were violent when the wife was better educated, compared with nine per cent when the husband was better educated or when they were equal.

## RISE ABOVE BIAS

The principal ways which others probe to categorise us in terms of class are:

- Accents
- Dress
- Education and
- Family background

Dress sense has already been discussed. Sociology professor Roy Boyne is right, however, when he says, 'The key signals the upper classes recognise are subtlety and quality. They use their dress sense to semaphore to each other. These signs are invisible to the uninitiated, but register clearly with those in the know.'

Education and family backgrounds are given – unless you choose to hide, or worse still, lie about them.

Accents are another matter. You can quite easily learn to tone down or lose completely regional or class-related dialects and vocabulary.

> **❝** *Less than 20% of adults are in the AB middle and upper classes* **❞**

To be upwardly mobile you will need to be able to win acceptance from people from higher social grades and you will find this is generally easier if you do not have a pronounced and stubbornly retained regional accent. There is no need to try and hide a dialect, and some danger in attempting to do so. But a softening more towards BBC standard English, accompanied by a wide vocabulary will help avoid the dangers of stereotypecasting. There are experts who can help with speech coaching, but the use of a cassette recorder and a little application should be adequate for most needs.

## WINNING THE SEX WAR

According to my dictionary a misogynist is defined as one who hates women. In my experience sexism in the workplace is more to do with men's fear of successful women than hatred of them.

Libby Purves writing in *The Times* summarised this well. 'The fact is that worried, pallid, conventional men of a certain age control most public media, and such men simply cannot abide extrovert, super-healthy, noisy women. When they think a big, tough, hearty woman is coming round the corner, these men cringe.'

Assertive women tend to attract the most prejudice. There is a Catch 22 situation at play here, because some women have become more assertive than their nature – may even have been on assertiveness courses – in order to cope with sexism at work. In this not uncommon scenario we have a complete stand-off situation.

If you find yourself at the wrong end of this you may decide to walk away from it. Changing an entire corporate culture or a lifelong bigot may call for your martyrdom. The alternative, if you do not feel too compromised, is to try and find a little common ground between the two of you. It might be a hobby, family circumstances, shared roots – something safe that will enable the two of you to lower your respective defences slightly and briefly.

With any luck you may find trace elements of a decent enough and probably insecure man, despite this particular character defect – and he may see you as a warmer human being who has made the effort, made the important first move. Should this tactic show any signs of success, restrict yourself, initially at least, to this one topic, keeping the rest of your relationship formal as before. Create a moment of intimacy with your customer (or boss) each day. That's all it needs to let people see there is more to you than efficiency and determination.

The definition I quoted of a misogynist – one who hates women – also covers another situation, and one that I think is more difficult. Women hating other women in business. It may be the result of a kind of inverted snobbery, or it may be as innocent a reason as not knowing how to behave because of the relative lack of role models for such situations. From my observations the best response to this problem is different from that just discussed. *Don't* try to establish bridgeheads. Instead let the more senior woman realise you know your place, acknowledge her status and are neither threatening it nor resentful of it. Don't become a Uriah Heep, but make it clear you understand the formalities of the relationship in terms of pecking order, and try to earn her respect by doing a good job – never by what may be regarded as guile. Hopefully, in time she will feel comfortable enough to relax and offer a bridgehead to you. However, be prepared for a long wait.

## SHRUGGING OFF SEX

Children learn to get their own way and win admiration by being cute, flirtatious and appealing. It is a lesson that can create many problems later in life, because in business these are social techniques which can lead to serious ambiguity in terms of the signals being sent.

There can be other reasons. Research conducted by Sara Figgs of Plymouth University Psychology Department showed that a staggering *79 per cent* of nurses had been sexually harassed by patients or colleagues. The very qualities which nurses are expected to possess – kindness, a caring approach, warmth, gentleness and friendliness – may well be the triggers which lead to the problem. 'I would suggest that a significant factor is that men wrongly perceive friendly, approachable behaviour as indicating sexual interest and availability,' says Ms Figgs.

Sixty per cent of women at work claim to have experienced sexual harassment. Drink releases inhibitions, impairs judgement and very often acts as a catalyst to this sort of behaviour.

Men can also be subject to sexual harassment at work. In a survey conducted by a men's health magazine in the USA, 57 per cent of readers reported that they had been sexually propositioned at work. Eighteen per cent said they had gone 'the whole way' at work with a female colleague.

In pulp fiction an office romance may seem fine – but real life sexuality does still shock and offend people. And there are no exceptions – even for the Christmas party or office outing.

My advice is to compartmentalise your business life and – other than those conscious and controlled moments of intimacy I have talked about – do not mix business with your social life. This is difficult where long hours are the norm. Do, however, search your behaviour patterns and ruthlessly expunge anything that could be seen as ambiguous to others. It's all part of our consistent theme of knowing yourself, and trying to see yourself as others see you.

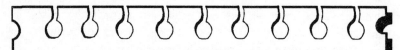

## SUMMARY

Prejudice is encountered to a greater or lesser degree in most business environments. *The 20% Factor* will help turn negatives into positives if you take the following action:

■ Reflect the values of the organisation

■ Don't mix sex and work

■ Become 20% more competent

■ Respect the pecking order.

# 6 BECOMING 20% MORE POPULAR

What follows is a package of insider's tips – often controversial – on how to get your way in business: The insider's *20% Factor*.

As we have seen, people who are liked get on far better than those who are not, and people who have a way with words also tend to come out on top. There are seven techniques you can use to encourage people to like you.

- Reconnaissance

- Look like them

- Be like them ('reflected responsing')

- Build the bridgehead

- Show deference

- Praise

- Third party influence

Being liked is important. Important to you in terms of your own morale and self-image. Important to your boss or customer, because research has shown a strong correlation between familiarity, favourability and success. We all prefer to deal with people (and organisations) we like.

We shall deal with each of these techniques in turn.

## 1. Reconnaissance
Find out all you can about the person (and organisation) who is important to you. Talk to people who know them and have worked with them. Try and understand the 'type' of person they are. A number of our earlier self-completion tests will have demonstrated how you can usefully categorise people into types.

In addition learn as much as you can about his or her organisation, the sector(s) in which it operates, his or her profession and training. Who is his or her boss, and what are they like? Visit their offices a few days before your interview or major meeting if you don't already know the organisation. Call in at the reception and request some literature, and use your eyes. See how people look, how they dress and the degree of formality.

Try and check out your key contact. Perhaps they are active in their trade association, or local Rotary club. What are their hobbies? Are they married – any children? Divorced?

Divorced people may be more cynical about life. The word 'divorcynic' was coined by researchers working on a project commissioned by Wasey-Campbell-Ewald from the Henley Centre and Holder Scorah. This research showed how divorcees were more sceptical than most about advertising and people selling to them. With nearly one in two marriages in the USA and one in three in the UK ending in divorce we are talking about large numbers. By the end of the century a quarter of all the people in the UK will have been affected by a broken marriage – with over half of divorces involving dependent children, and over half remarrying.

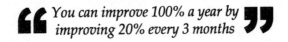
**ᶜᶜ** *You can improve 100% a year by improving 20% every 3 months* **ᴶᴶ**

When you meet new important people for the first time, notice their office. Is it tidy or chaotic? Look for personal mementoes – sports cups, pictures of the family, boat, with the Prime Minister, framed certificates of membership of associations, attendance at training courses or awards.

The purpose of all of this is twofold:

■ To help you feel more confident from being on top of the situation, in possession of the facts.

■ To help you select one or two topics to create a 'bridgehead'.

'Reconnaissance', 'bridgehead' – these are deliberately terms with an army ring. I think these parallels are appropriate because what I am trying to stress is the military planning, single-mindedness and professionalism you need to succeed.

### 2. Look like them
The information from your reconnaissance should have given you a good idea of the kind of people who are going to get on with

this person, and those who will jar. The self-completion exercises later in the book will help you think scientifically about these things (conservative *v* radical; Machiavelli *v* Pangloss; maximiser *v* minimiser etc).

When you meet them, present yourself as 'their kind of person'. This includes dress sense and the degree of formality most appropriate.

### 3. Be like them – 'reflected responsing'

Be an active listener: we all like people who are good listeners; and it will help you refine the skill of 'reflected responsing'. This encompasses some tried and tested basic psychological techniques. For example, as an active (rather than passive) listener, you will be able to spot cues to enable you to nod and feed back mutual views and values to the other person. Don't use the same words of course, simply find another way of phrasing what they have been saying. Or offer any anecdote that you are confident will echo back their values and opinions.

---

#### HOW INTERESTING!

Be a good listener and you'll be thought to be very bright and fascinating. Therapist Mary Edwardes, when married to tycoon Sir Michael Edwardes, had to attend many dinners with important people. At one, she told *The Mail on Sunday*, she was sat next to a senior civil servant. 'At the start I asked him what it was like to have his job and he proceeded to talk uninterrupted for two and a half hours.

'The next day he happened to see Michael and complimented him on having such an interesting wife.'

---

If you are a good listener and skilled at reflecting back the other person's views, you'll be surprised how interesting and intelligent they will find you. Under no circumstances directly or even obliquely disagree with them. On those occasions when you are unsure of what to say, use the psychiatrist's tactic of batting back a non-contentious gambit. If, for example, they are complaining about interest rates or a strong pound you might say, 'You feel the Government could do more to help.' This shows you are listening and buys you more time to grasp the point. Your reflected responses should be put as *statements* not questions.

The same techniques should be used in body language. If they use a lot of eye contact, you should adopt the same. Research psychologist Dr David Lewis suggests that a man dealing with another man should maintain eye contact for between 60–70 per cent of the time. Less than that and you may seem to them shifty and insecure, more than that may be seen as aggressive. A man to woman ratio is around 50 per cent. A woman dealing fairly assertively with a man should be back to the 70 per cent level.

---

### KIDNAPPERS

Avoiding eye contact with threatening individuals is good advice. I generally take a window seat on planes on the basis that any hijackers would find it easier to pick on someone in an aisle seat first!

But if an abduction does take place there will probably be a need to be submissive to the aggressor. Experts in this field describe the Stockholm Factor, where the person abducted develops a close supportive relationship with the abductor.

It is a fact that well-developed interpersonal skills can, in extreme hostage-style crises, help save your life. The top police negotiators in this field could probably become business or political leaders if they channelled their skills in a different direction

---

To maximise rapport hold eye contact when the other person begins talking, and always break contact downwards. An upward glance will suggest lack of interest and may be taken as a deliberate insult. One useful tip is to ensure the other person has eye contact with you when you are making a strong point or are about to try and close a sale. You will achieve far more impact if you look them full in the eye at such key moments. Use a prop – a pen, your spectacles, or just

---

### EYE CONTACT

Eye contact is the most immediate signal we give out and receive in meetings. Weighing people up – eyeing people up – is of course all part of any new encounter. But we should realise that eyes can and often do immediately establish a friendly or hostile relationship, or a dominant or submissive role.

Research, pioneered by Professor Eckhard Hess when he was working with Chicago University, suggests that the degree of dilation of a person's eyes can give out receptive (pupils wide) or non-receptive (small dilation) signals. In an experiment a man was shown two photographs of women who were identical twins. When asked which one he found to be most attractive he indicated the woman whose pupils were enlarged, without knowing why. In the eighteenth century it was not unusual for society women to use the drug atropine to enlarge their pupils to make themselves more attractive to men, and when sitting for portraits.

your hand touching your temple – to direct their eyes into your own, and then let them have your message with both barrels!

If the other person is leaning forward attentively, do the same. If they cross their arms, or cross their legs, do the same – not too obviously, of course. The same goes for jackets being worn on or off. But at all times remain clearly attentive in terms of posture and general demeanour. Never fold your arms, for example – this creates a barrier – and never lean back or slouch, even if they do.

---

### PETRUSHKA

One of the greatest artistic performances I have enjoyed was David Bintley dancing Petrushka at Covent Garden. Dance is simply another example of body language and in Petrushka words become completely redundant as the beautiful doll, the bullying Turk and the sad, little toy clown Petrushka come to life as puppets after dark, while the children are sleeping.

---

Make sure that you have no nervous habits which may unconsciously demonstrate boredom with or dislike of the other person. Ask friends and partners openly if you have any such habits – nose scratching, ear lobe pulling, finger drumming, irritating throat clearing – and expunge them ruthlessly. As Sigmund Freud said, 'If his lips are silent, he chatters with his fingertips: betrayal oozes out of him at every pore.'

The effect of all of this advice is to help the other person feel unthreatened and comfortable with you, for intangible reasons. It also reduces the risk of irrational alienation and helps you remain quietly in control. This even extends to the physical distance we stand or sit from one another. For the British, northern Europeans and East Coast Americans, a distance of eighteen inches to two feet is fairly intimate and should be reserved for close friends and family. From experience, two and a half feet to maybe as much as four feet seems to me about right for business contacts and strangers.

To experiment with this phenomenon you can have fun trying the cocktail party waltz. Stand a foot too close to some stranger with whom you find yourself talking, and you will see that he or she will move back to establish a comfortable distance. Invade their space again and you can begin to waltz them around the room towards somebody you find more interesting.

My experience is that people from the Southern and Middle Eastern countries – Italians, Greeks, Spanish, Arabs, Israelis, Latin Americans and indeed West Coast Americans – generally have a close tolerance level and touch more. The Japanese are far less tactile and need even more space than the British. I also find the Japanese far less comfortable with the 60–70 per cent of eye contact described. Fifty per cent or less seems more appropriate.

You are beginning to develop your encoding and decoding skills. Try your hand at a psychology test to see how skilled you might be as a counsellor using reflective responding. It is taken (with kind permission) from case material which appeared in Norman R Maier and Gertrude Casselman Verser's book *Psychology in Industrial Organisations* (Fifth Edition, © 1982, Houghton Mifflin Company). Turn to pages 67–72: select the best response.

In an examination about 13 per cent of students made no errors in this exercise. Twenty three per cent made one error; 43 per cent two or three errors; 14 per cent four to six mistakes; and 7 per cent made seven or more errors.

Questions 8, 10 and 4 were found the most difficult – in that order, and 9, 1, and 12 the least difficult.

### 4. Build the bridgehead

Your reconnaissance and your active listening should have identified for you something that may help you create the 'moment of intimacy' with the other person I spoke about earlier. Obvious topics of seemingly common interest may be regional origins, shared educational experiences, children, schools, sport, the arts or a mutual hobby. In any event always be prepared with three or four possible topics for a little pre- or post-meeting small talk – events in the news, significant national or world affairs. These can be used to help fill any awkward gaps or silences.

The intention is to help you find some safe moment of intimacy with the person. One common device used to help make friends with someone is to share a secret with them: it makes that person feel special and trusted. This moment of intimacy touches a similar human need to be seen as a special *individual*.

### 5. Show deference

Your role with someone important to you in career terms should be submissive and attentive – at least in the early stages of a new relationship. My master/servant role-playing advice is based on

# Reflected response assessment ☑

| Remark | Select best response to reflect |
|---|---|
| 1. The client has been on a new team for 3 months. During a counselling interview he said 'I don't know why it is, but I just don't feel as though I'm one of the gang. They are all nice enough fellows, but somehow they seem to have a closed circle and make me feel like an outsider. Maybe it's me; I don't know.' | a  Why don't you use the first chance you get to do the boys a favour?<br><br>b  It seems to you that the group doesn't accept you.<br><br>c  It seems that the others dislike you for some reason.<br><br>d  You don't think they will accept you if you give them some more time to learn that you are a nice fellow. |
| 2. Client is a 20-year-old male. He states, 'God, I hate my mum. She tries to run my life for me. I feel almost as strongly about my dad. He just sits back and lets her run everything, and never protests.' | a  You feel the father should be stronger than the mother.<br><br>b  You resent your mother for being too strong, and your father for being too weak.<br><br>c  You feel guilty because you can't accept the idea that you hate your parents.<br><br>d  Getting away from home for a while would relieve the immediate tension and give you a chance to work out this problem. |

| Remark | Select best response to reflect |
|---|---|
| 3. A clerical employee with 10 years' experience told his supervisor: 'I've been doing this job for years now and nobody had ever complained and now you send my work back and tell me to do it again. It isn't fair and it doesn't make sense. Maybe I do make mistakes now and then, but nobody is perfect and I don't know why I should get all the blame for what goes on around here.' | a It isn't fair to ask you to correct your own mistakes. b Suppose you check your work before you bring it to me. c You think you are being blamed for not being perfect. d You feel that I am too strict. |
| 4. The following statement was made by a patient during a counselling session: 'There is nothing wrong with me. I only came to see you because my doctor insisted upon it.' | a That may be true, but shall we wait and see? b You are resentful about coming here. c You really don't want to be here. d What do you think was his reason for sending you here? |

| Remark | Select best response to reflect |
|---|---|
| 5. During an interview with his supervisor, a member of a team states: 'I don't want to work with Jake any more. He's lazy and is always taking a superior attitude and complains about the rest of us not helping him as much as we should. He thinks he is too good for this kind of work and too good to work with the rest of us and I'm sick of being around him.' | a You feel that Jake ought to be disciplined in some way.<br><br>b Jake doesn't want to cooperate, is that it?<br><br>c Jake's attitude makes the work unpleasant.<br><br>d You think Jake might fit in better somewhere else. |
| 6. A young man whose work showed a sudden drop in quality was sent to the employment manager for an interview. One of the things he said on arriving was: 'I don't know why I should be asked to talk to you about my work. I haven't complained and I haven't time for this kind of chit-chat. So give me what help you have in mind and I'll be on my way.' | a You came to see me because you were sent and not because you feel any need for help.<br><br>b Don't you feel that with my experience in the company I might be of some help?<br><br>c You feel irritated for coming here because you don't think I can help you.<br><br>d You mustn't jump to conclusions. Often people need help when they are unaware of this need. |

| | Remark | Select best response to reflect |
|---|---|---|
| 7. | Man – age 59: 'I couldn't let my son help me now that I'm down and out. I've got that shred of pride left – because you see I remember when he was a kid and I didn't turn my hand to help him. I traipsed around the country – his mother died when the kid was born – and I let the relatives push him around and stuck him in foster homes – and now – it certainly was like a knife stuck in me when we met the other day and he said, "We can make a go of it together, Dad – I've got a little money saved up." No – No – I won't let him do it. I will clear out of here. It'll be hard – but – I haven't done one thing for him – or anyone else for that matter.' | a What was your married life like? Had you and your wife planned for a child? <br><br> b Have you thought what it will mean to your son if you don't let him do this thing which he wants to do for you? <br><br> c I see what you mean. You feel that you don't deserve the help he wants to give because in the past you did nothing to earn it. And your statement that you never have done anything for anyone else makes it look as if it might be a real problem for you to accept responsibility for helping others, and to accept help from others. <br><br> d Your behaviour in the past makes you unworthy of the help your son wants to give you now, is that what you mean? |
| 8. | In the middle of a counselling interview, an 18-year-old girl who became emotionally disturbed after an operation on her face, spoke as follows: 'A person can't spend a lifetime hating someone as badly and completely as I hate my mother and not have it tear their nerves to pieces. As long as I can remember I have hated her and wished she would die. She was so dominating, she killed my father. She drove him to suicide. I – I found her. She is like a vampire – sucking the life's blood out of her children. The plastic surgery was incidental. I have been used since I was a child as a convenient housemaid. Mother was starting a business of her own. She was a dynamic power. Every energy she had was poured into making a success. And she did. She has a chain of stores now. And all of us remaining children have money in our own names. She wants us to help in the business. One of my sisters is a partner now. Another sister got married, and when Tom didn't "fit in", Mother caused a separation and now Louise is home – brooding, but docile. Now she wants me to take over another branch. And won't she be surprised when she discovers that the minute I'm twenty-one out comes my money and away I go, never to return again.' | a You feel that the best solution is to take your money and run away from home. <br><br> b Your life has been made unbearable by your mother's domination and your feelings toward her make it impossible for you to go into business with her. <br><br> c Is it not possible that you will feel guilty if you make a rash decision at this time? <br><br> d All of us feel like that at one time or another. You must not let your feelings get the best of you. |

| Remark | Select best response to reflect |
|---|---|
| 9. Man – age 41: "I've been married four times and each time I've thought, 'Boy, this is the real thing!' None of them has ever been like this girl. She's the most beautiful girl you ever saw – and dance! And she dresses like a million dollars. She's out of this world!' | a You're really enthusiastic about her. <br><br> b How does she compare with your other wives? How did you feel about them before you married? <br><br> c If she's anything like you seem to feel she is, she must be quite a catch. Maybe this time you'll stick. <br><br> d Doesn't it strike you as odd that every time you've felt the same way? |
| 10. Man – age 35: "I'm determined to get ahead. I'm not afraid of hard work. I am not afraid to take a few hard knocks – if I can see my goal out there in front. And I'm not adverse to climbing over a few people – who get in my way – because this means a lot to me. I can't be satisfied with just a mediocre job. No, I want to be somebody.' | a You feel that you just have to be out on top no matter what you may do to others. <br><br> b You see yourself as a deeply ambitious person, is that it? <br><br> c What do you suppose is behind this strong determination of yours to get ahead? <br><br> d Strong ambition can be a real asset to any man. Are you really sure, though, that you mean it when you say you're not adverse to climbing over those who get in your way? Couldn't that turn out to do you more harm than good? |

| Remark | Select best response to reflect |
|--------|--------------------------------|
| 11. Man – age 29: 'I keep remembering how I walked out on Mary and the two kids. Five years ago – the law never caught up with me – I thought I was pretty smart – but now – God, but I was a heel. I don't see how I could do it. And I'm so ashamed I can't look people in the eye. Now I can't find her – not a trace. Her relatives won't tell me where she is. I don't blame them – but how could I have done it? Just because it was tough going. I tell you, I'll never have any self-respect. Never! And I – I don't know what to do – or how I can even try to rectify my big mistake. I don't know –!' | a There are a number of things you might do to try to find her. You could list her as a missing person and get police help. You could get a private detective agency to handle it for you. You might even be able to get a court order that would force the relatives to give her address.<br><br>b When did you decide that you wanted her back? Tell me the circumstances.<br><br>c The hopelessness there seems pretty clearly connected with the feelings of guilt.<br><br>d As you see it then, your behaviour is just plain unforgivable. |
| 12. A secretary, began to cry when asked whether or not she had finished typing a first draft of a speech the personnel director was preparing and said: 'Everything I do is wrong. I just can't do anything to please you. I don't mind when you criticise me to my face but when you start writing me up as if I were a case – a good joke – well, I just can't take it.' (Assume that the speech included a humorous anecdote about a secretary.) | a There is no reference to you as a person in that speech.<br><br>b You feel I criticise you too publicly.<br><br>c I'll be glad to take that out, but aren't you being a bit sensitive?<br><br>d You feel I'm making fun of you in that story. |

Correct responses: 1-b, 2-b, 3-c, 4-c, 5-c, 6-a, 7-d, 8-b, 9-a, 10-a, 11-d, 12-d the theory that people with power and authority welcome unprompted recognition of the distinction. It lightens the need for them to use difficult value judgements on how far they have openly to assert that authority. Indeed there is evidence from some psychologists that successful relationships generally can best be built upon some degree of dominance from one party and submissiveness from the other.

In 1952 Dr Robert Winch published his work *The Modern Family* in which he reflected the view that the key to some successful marriages and other close partnerships was one person complementing the more dominant other person. This has seemed to me an equally accurate observation of some of the most successful business teams.

One of the claims made by some historians, Geoffrey Best for example, for the peace and economic prosperity of Britain in the mid-Victorian years 1851–75 was the deference showed by the various strata of classes to their 'betters'. This is well illustrated in the (now outlawed) verse of that famous hymn *All Things Bright and Beautiful*:

> The rich man in his castle,
> The poor man at his gate,
> God made them, high or lowly,
> And order'd their estate.

Deference today should not be confused with servility. It remains

---

### SEND THE RIGHT SIGNALS

Once on a business trip to India, I had some important packages tied up in the truly Kafka-esque bureaucracy at Delhi Airport. It was proving impossible to get them cleared through customs. After hours of negotiating with a local agent, we had gone past official closing time and the following day customs was to be closed for a religious holiday.

Despite the late hour we went to the final point of clearance one last desperate time. My agent's ferocious arguing in Hindi was getting us nowhere. Then I caught the attention of the official, established eye contact, muttered something about please help us, and performed the Indian gesture for please – hands held stiffly before the face in prayer form, and then the head and shoulders bowed.

He watched me carefully, and searched my eyes to see if I was being facetious. When he saw I was in earnest, and genuinely submissive, he suddenly grinned, stamped the form, and I finally got my packages.

---

### A GOOD TIP

A friend of mine tells the story of when he waited on tables for a while in a top and rather posh hotel restaurant, where the head waiter had something of a reputation for keeping up proprieties. Virtually every other day a local solicitor would use the restaurant for lunching various clients, and each time he was rude and left very mean tips. One day, when the restaurant was especially full, the two men were just leaving when the head waiter bellowed: 'Excuse me, gentlemen. You seem to have left your bus fares on the table.' Other diners burst into laughter and the man never returned.

Hardly great customer relations you might think. But if this chap had been souring the ambience of the restaurant and making his waiters miserable for years, it really was a shrewd move to drive him away. What it also was, of course, was a very big and public 'thank you' to his own staff.

---

a powerful influence – when used knowingly and skilfully – along with praise and ingratiation.

### 6. Praise

Just as deference is an unfashionable yet still potent brew, no less so is ingratiation and praise.

Everyone likes praise, and even flattery. As discussed earlier, bosses should praise much more – and not just the high achievers. They know they are doing well. It is the conscientious, reliable 'plodder' who most values recognition.

The following chart shows the effect of praise and reprimand on the work of US college students. It was modified by Norman Maier in *Psychology in Industrial Organisations* (fifth edition, © 1982, Houghton Mifflin Company. Used with permission) from H Moore's 'Psychology For Business And Industry'.

Praise improved work in 87.5 per cent of students whilst at the other extreme, public sarcasm lead to poorer results in 65.1 per cent of students. In fact only one method of disapproval – private reprimand – resulted in a greater balance doing better.

Praise *works*. However, praise is normally associated with being given from the top down, whereas it can work even better in the other direction. Bosses and important people enjoy praise and flattery no less than anyone else – and perhaps more. The best tactic is to praise the *results* of their performances rather than giving some clumsy compliment to them as individuals. Again, your reconnaissance will give you some pointers. For example, if they have written an article for a trade paper, or spoken at a conference, you can say how much you agreed with what they said: this acts as a double compliment. First, you have read what they said, recognising their celebrity – and second, you are agreeing with them. If their market share has risen under their stewardship, or if their latest financial results were good, remark on it flatteringly but knowledgeably.

## Comparison of positive and negative incentives

| Incentive | Order of merit | Percentage showing: | | |
| --- | --- | --- | --- | --- |
| | | Better results | Same results | Poorer results |
| Public praise | 1 | 87.5 | 12.0 | 0.5 |
| Private reprimand | 2 | 66.3 | 23.0 | 10.7 |
| Public reprimand | 3 | 34.7 | 26.7 | 38.7 |
| Private ridicule | 4 | 32.5 | 33.0 | 34.5 |
| Public ridicule | 5 | 17.0 | 35.7 | 47.3 |
| Private sarcasm | 6 | 27.9 | 27.5 | 44.7 |
| Public sarcasm | 7 | 11.9 | 23.0 | 65.1 |

## 7. Third party influence

This is more difficult to achieve, but can be one of the most powerful devices with which to make yourself popular. Try to engineer a situation whereby a third party either says positive things about you to your boss, or reports you saying positive things about your boss to them.

As an adolescent there was nothing more guaranteed to attract your attention than to hear someone of the opposite sex telling you how much their friend found you attractive. It's the same in business.

Third party endorsement is especially powerful because it introduces some degree of objectivity into the evaluation of people and it makes you privy to a flattering secret. Powerful stuff.

## BAD IMPRESSIONS – AND HOW TO AVOID THEM

First impressions matter, but worst impressions will remain in people's memories and are virtually impossible to dislodge. Once somebody sees you at your worst you will always be typecast in that way by that person.

There are two potential causes of worst impressions:

■ Your own stupidity or weakness

■ Your inability to cope well in a crisis.

### Stupidity

Most worst impressions stem from people being caught off-guard, relaxing and becoming informal or over-familiar. Drink impairs judgements and is often to blame. A tonic and bitters, low alcohol beer or white wine and soda is a good idea at formal and informal gatherings of people with whom you have working relationships. That one drink too many can be the catalyst that leads to any number of horrors – the compulsive urge to tell bad taste jokes, swearing, becoming indiscrete or aggressive or pathetically self-pitying.

Worse still is the temptation to hint at or make sexual advances, wanted or not. Few reputations can survive the knowledge or suspicion of a sexual adventurer bubbling away under a calm exterior. One damning coded warning is that he or she is NSIT – not safe in taxis!

The answer is to take a grip on yourself and avoid these obvious and avoidable alcoholic and sexual pitfalls. All your months and years of hard work spent winning confidence and respect can be dashed against these well charted reefs. We all remember people at their worst, or descriptions – suitably embroidered – of them from others.

Maria Callas was a supreme artiste loved and respected around the world. Many of us, however, are unable to get out of our minds an unflattering Associated Press photograph of her which was front paged in November 1955. She had just been served with a summons in her dressing room at the Chicago Opera House by Marshal Stanley Pringle and Deputy Sheriff Dan Smith after her performance in Madame Butterfly. Still in her Cio-Cio-San kimono she was lost in rage and her snarling graceless picture still leaps to my mind after all these years when I think of her.

Photographs can capture people at their worst or most foolish. A photograph used by Harold Evans in his book *Pictures on a Page* (William Heinemann, London, 1978) shows a girl kneeling over her boyfriend on a beach. He had almost died from drowning and a photographer had tried to capture the tragic scene. In fact the girl, looking up and seeing the photographer, automatically smiled through years of conditioning to smile at cameras. This is not the girl's fault of course. But so often the cause of projecting a bad or inappropriate image is our own foolishness.

## COPING WITH CRISIS

Our reaction to a crisis is more difficult to manage. Crises of any kind can bring out the worst or best in people – normally one extreme or the other – and this will always paint the most memorable picture in our minds.

In the home or office, a small fire, discovering a burglar, a medical crisis – someone choking, fainting, needing a tourniquet – in these unplanned, unrehearsed emergencies any veneer of urbanity and control can be stripped away, and you may act like a coward or panic. Somerset Maugham caught such a moment perfectly in his short story *The Door Of Opportunity*.

Preparation and understanding of what is going on around you will help you to cope. At the time of the blitz during the Second World War, research in London suggested that children were not really afraid of the bangs, flashes and shudders from the bombs. Two factors had a much greater bearing – separation from their mothers, and the degree of anxiety communicated by the mother. If she was calm, so were her children.

Crises are the most difficult times for the 15–30 per cent of UK adults who have a minor mental illness, half of which last for less than 12 months, almost all of whom make a full recovery. Mental and stress related illnesses cost British business around £7 billion a year – the equivalent of 80 million lost working days. The most common mental illness is anxiety and depression, caused by boredom, overwork, constant change of activity, lack of praise or recognition, repetitive work, promotion, lack of fulfilment, lack of personal contact and poor conditions. Therapy is now widely available and happily much of society's stigma has gone. Many employers – with the active support of the Department of Health and the Confederation of British Industry – have put into place mental health programmes. These cover workplace counselling schemes, education, encouragement for use of external counselling services, employee assistance programmes, self-help classes and a range of preventative measures.

---

### CAN YOU KEEP A SECRET?

When I was policy co-ordinator to the president of the Confederation of British Industry I was given a piece of information by an overseas agency, which seemed to me to be of the most extreme international importance. They used it as an inducement to meet me. I smelled an entrapment so passed on the details to the Foreign Office and another agency. But for the weeks I carried that secret around with me, I felt I would burst – wanting to tell everyone.

Years later when it was safe, I was able to do just that, and used the incident as a basis for my second espionage novel, *Seward's Folly* (Methuen, 1980, London).

---

Panic attacks are suffered by over 3 per cent of people, and on occasions all of us have let our nerves get the better of us. Symptoms range from a blushing and blotchy necks, sweating, palpitations, red spots before the eyes, ringing in the ears, vomiting, uncontrollable weeping or grizzling, loss of control of the bowels and bladder, and possibly blackouts. Hardly things which will impress upon those around you that you have leadership qualities.

People suffering from the terrible condition of severe panic attacks should also seek therapy. The rest of us can help ourselves by a combination of measures – more preparation and rehearsal (fire drills, taking lessons in self-defence, studying first aid and so on) and by desensitivising ourselves from the fear by deliberately exposing ourselves to it (getting back on the horse that threw you; overcoming the fear of flying by understanding more about planes and their procedures – what the different engine noises mean and so on). We should also train ourselves to be *positive thinkers*, concentrating on things which will go right, rather than things which *may* (or may not) go wrong.

Confront fear and think positive!

## INTERVIEW YOURSELF

As we come towards the end of Part 2 – A 20% Better You, I would like you to consider the rather personal ground we have just covered and attempt to be brutally honest about how your current or potential employers see you. I am asking you to put your best face forward, of course – so perhaps you should carry out this exercise in the context of the 'new' 20% better you.

### The Five Point Plan

A useful way to discipline your way of business thinking is to use a framework commonly applied (in a systemised or intuitive way) by employers when interviewing people. I want you to use the widely adopted Five Point Plan to interview *yourself*. You cannot be really objective about yourself of course, but it should prove to be a useful way to order your thoughts about yourself and others.

When using the Five Point Plan give marks on a scale of ten for the following five headings:

1. **First impressions**: This covers that first impact we have been discussing. What 'type' of person, this is relative to the 'type' of person I need. All the elements of dress sense, hair, age, class and immediate chemistry are factors here.

2. **Qualifications**: The person's curriculum vitae (CV) will already have told me whether he or she has a degree, post graduate or professional diploma. But I'll want to probe a little more about school activities, why they chose a certain degree or subject to study, why they chose a certain university or college.

3. **Background**: In addition to qualifications I'll want to know more about the kind of environment in which they grew up. Which town, what did their parents do for a living, do they have brothers or sisters, or are they an only child? An indication of their religious and political roots is also helpful.

   If they come from a poor background are they angry, embarrassed or proud of it? If from a wealthy background are they down-to-earth or snooty; did they cope well with, say, boarding or did they (like many) have a miserable time that has left permanent scars? What do their spouse/partner/ friends do for their living?

4. **Motivation**: What drives this person? Are they ruthlessly ambitious or modestly so? Are they looking for rapid promotion and status (which might mean they see my company as a calculated stepping stone for higher things elsewhere), or are they looking for steady, medium-term commitment? Perhaps their real passion lies outside work – are they competitive sportsmen or women, single figure golf handicappers, contemporary dance fanatics or people who only come to life when talking about their children or stamp collection?

5. **Aptitude**: Do they have the skills and approach actually to do the job? Sometimes you can test aspects of this – typing, proof reading and spelling, ability with numbers, writing and presentation skills, and for some job dexterity. Mostly, though, you have to form your own opinion, based in part by looking at the portfolio of work they have done for other people and purposes – either in another job, or at college or in terms of hobbies/outside interests. I will also ask myself whether they are strategists – capable of seeing the wider, overall picture – or tacticians.

---

### HOME GOALS

If you have achieved the painstaking and difficult task of winning the confidence of your boss or big customer my advice is to avoid involving them with your home life, for example by inviting them round for dinner.

Suddenly your partner, your children and your taste in furniture, music and food will be thrust in front of them – with *their* spouse, who will become another less predictable arbiter on everything about you. Unless you are exceptionally socially confident, *don't do it.* And politely avoid invitations to their home.

Why do you think some large corporations create forums to meet spouses of potential fast track managers? It's a way of double-checking you, of looking behind that carefully constructed image that has served you so well to date. Try and avoid it. The risks outweigh any benefits.

---

Those, then, are the components of the Five Point Plan – shown on page 82. As you can see, it is not too difficult to interview yourself using this technique. Imagine you are presenting yourself for an interview for a specific, interesting job (find one advertised in a newspaper). Decide how you would dress for it, and how you would respond to the kinds of questions you can predict they may ask. At the same time have in your mind the kind of organisation which has run the job advertisement. You will need to have a feel for their sort of culture – small company/thrusting and ambitious; more conservative large old company etc, what industry sector it's in and the prevailing culture there (eg a software house will be very different from a firm of patents agents or a local government department).

Having formed these guesses (make them educated guesses by doing a little research into the company) you should make yourself as close as you humanly can to the type of person you think they want.

So find a newspaper, find that interesting job ad and start the process of research. Then interview yourself.

Once you have completed the Five Point Plan, double your marks to give a score out of a hundred. If you have a colleague whose judgement you trust, you might ask him or her to repeat the exercise by 'interviewing' you. Then compare the marks.

This same procedure takes place in one form or another almost every day in businesses. Not just during job interviews, but in how you impact on your customers, potential customers, your bosses or existing or new people who may report to you.

Really work hard, first, to know yourself and your range of experience, and second, to find out what it is others want from you, so that you can package whatever you have to offer especially for them.

Don't worry that somehow you will become corporately schizophrenic. The differences, although very subtle, are nonetheless potentially very influential.

# Interviewing: the Five Point Plan ☑

|  | Your assessment of yourself for a named job | A colleague's assessment of you for the named job |
|---|---|---|
| **First impressions:** dress, size, hair, deportment, accent, age, 'chemistry' etc |  |  |
| **Qualifications:** school, college/university, professional, other (eg hobbies taken to exam standard – piano etc), languages |  |  |
| **Background:** where born, lives, parents' occupations, family roots – religion, politics, peer group's jobs |  |  |
| **Motivation:** money or status, power or security, very ambitious or plodder, any powerful outside passions, eg sport, amateur dramatics |  |  |
| **Aptitude:** portfolio of other work, performance in any proof reading, mathematical, writing tests etc you may set |  |  |
| **Total of scores**<br>**X 2 = %** |  |  |

Once you have completed the Five Point Plan on yourself, and possibly with a friend's help too, imagine how another person you know well (perhaps the same friend) would score for that same job.

This is part of an important programme of exercises. What we are doing is beginning to train and discipline you to decide what others want from you, and to know the extent to which you can meet that need by a little fine tuning: *The 20% Factor*.

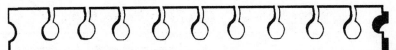

## SUMMARY

20% more effort can result in 100% more positive
reaction from your colleagues:

- Improve interpersonal skills
- See yourself as others see you
- Maintain your self-respect
- Confront fear and think positive!

# PART 2 CHECKLIST

- Your appearance will have a major influence on your chances of success

- Keep business dress simple and smart – ordinariness is a key component of attractiveness

- Personality matters more than inherited physical characteristics

- Reflect your organisation's values

- 55 per cent of the impact we make is based on appearance, 38 per cent on presentation and only 7 per cent on what we actually say

- Good health and vitality will convey the best first impression

- The right approach can overcome prejudice

- Avoid mixing business and social life

- Worst impressions last

- Preparation and knowledge can help you avoid – or cope with – a crisis

- See yourself as your employers see you

- Popularity breeds success!

# A

# 20%

# BETTER MANAGER

In Parts 1 and 2 we learned the need to know ourselves, our limitations and how to make the most of our strengths.

In Part 3 we will begin to apply all of this to improving our performance as managers. To achieve this we must understand – *really* understand – what it is that our employers want from us, and how they will judge us.

This is the simple and consistent message of *The 20% Factor*. Find out what people want, and give it to them. Already armed with a clearer idea of what we have to offer as individuals, it is time now to decide how best to package ourselves. And the first step is to understand what does and does not work in your own organisation. To do this we have to understand organisations as well as we now know ourselves.

# 7 KNOW YOUR OWN ORGANISATION

All organisations – like individuals – have unique personalities and cultures. Sometimes this is stamped on them by a charismatic founder or chief executive; sometimes it has simply evolved over time, but is normally heavily influenced by the sector in which it operates. Very often we lump, quite unfairly, all companies in certain sectors together and assume that, for example, all banks and insurance companies operate in a very similar way, all food manufacturers are the same, all local government authorities, all firms of accountants etc.

The next assessment chart will test how well you match your organisation by creating personality profiles for both. For you to do well in the organisation your personality profiles should be broadly similar. The main exception would be if a CEO had been just appointed to shake the place up and make changes. The rest of us, however, generally ought to conform.

## Personality profiles assessment ☑

All you have to do is rate yourself on the sixteen qualities listed. You will see there are ten dots which separate the adjectives on the left side from the adjectives at the other end of the scale on the right. Decide for each where you lie between the two, on a scale of 1–10, and put a small cross on the appropriate dot.

Next, use a different coloured pen and do the same exercise, this time judging the personality of your organisation. If you imagine those qualities which characterise your corporation were embodied in a single individual, you should have no difficulties in scoring this assessment. Then, once more, place a small cross at a point on the dotted line which shows the extent to which your company reflects a particular attribute.

Finally connect each set of crosses, using different coloured pens.

Notice where your profile and that of your organisation corresponds. Ask yourself how important those attributes on which you diverge are to you. Major differences in attitude and approach can produce frustration, anxiety and depression. If you and your organisation are mismatched either you must change (the most likely scenario unless *you* are the new boss) or you should consider whether you are likely to reach your full potential within that organisation as it stands.

---

### Personality profiles assessment

I am

My company is

| Conservative | . . . . . . . . . | Radical |
| Tough-minded | . . . . . . . . . | Tender-hearted |
| Perfectionist | . . . . . . . . . | Casual |
| Orthodox | . . . . . . . . . | Unorthodox |
| Thrusting | . . . . . . . . . | Diffident |
| Confident | . . . . . . . . . | Uncertain |
| Determined | . . . . . . . . . | Hesitant |
| Painstaking | . . . . . . . . . | Slapdash |
| Predatory | . . . . . . . . . | Passive |
| Traditional | . . . . . . . . . | Innovative |
| Inflexible | . . . . . . . . . | Flexible |
| Practical | . . . . . . . . . | Impractical |
| Go ahead | . . . . . . . . . | Hidebound |
| Responsible | . . . . . . . . . | Irresponsible |
| Moral | . . . . . . . . . | Unethical |
| Energetic | . . . . . . . . . | Lethargic |

---

Next, conduct a Do It Yourself communications audit on your own organisation. This will help you consider how open it is, and who it sees as its most important influencers.

## The DIY communications audit

Make a haphazard list of all the people with whom your company communicates. It will be a long list, and will include all or most of the following:

- customers
- suppliers
- employees
- trade unions
- shareholders/the City
- the local community
- bankers
- the taxman
- your trade association
- 'the media'
- local government
- MPs/MEPs/peers
- civil servants
- industry analysts.

These are the target audiences for your various communications. Next prioritise the list into, say, the top three target audiences. Unless you have some pressing environmental or political problem these are likely to include:

- customers
- shareholders/the City
- employees.

It soon becomes clear that these broad headings are not adequate. Analyse each further:

**Customers:** for many businesses customers will broadly categorise into key accounts/the major national and regional multiples, and the independents. They may be further broken down by sales territories, by credit and non-credit customers. Also for the key accounts there may be a pecking order within each customer – the day to day buyer you deal with, his buying director, and his senior general management. Each will need a different style and frequency of communication from you. Then there are existing customers, lapsed customers, and customers from whom you would like to get a listing; there are domestic customers, export customers and agents.

List how you currently communicate with your various customer audiences:

- sales calls
- key account meetings
- sales conference for buyers
- trade and consumer advertising
- mailers/catalogues/price up-dates
- presentations to customer's own sales conferences
- through the trade press and national media
- through trade associations, industry seminars and conferences
- trade shows and exhibitions
- through planned hospitality etc.

Estimate how much all this communication costs you in terms of management time, print and production, conference and exhibition stand costs, and the rest. Then put yourself in the shoes of a key buyer and rank the various methods of communication in order of influence and importance. If he were asked by one of your research people what form of supplier communication he finds most important, what would he say? And what tone and style work best? Is it the big-production-number pushy sales conference, is it the trade show stand you agonise over, or is it a couple of businesslike meetings to talk turkey followed by some phone calls?

**Shareholders/the City:** this target audience may include institutional shareholders, smaller private shareholders, the banks, stockbrokers and other City analysts, the Stock Exchange, divisions, employees and, of course, the City press.

List how you currently communicate with these important audiences:

- full year and interim results, annual report and AGM, employees' report
- chairman's briefings
- periodic presentations to fund managers, bankers and analysts
- on and off the record briefings on the company and the sector for brokers' analysts
- through City press comment
- trade, consumer or any corporate/City advertising.

Ask how well this is all working and how prepared you would be, for example, to defend a hostile bid. If you are publicly owned, when did you last inspect your register of shareholders? Have you monitored it for any significant changes? What percentage of the shares are in the hands of institutions? As for the private shareholders, have you analysed how long each shareholder has held them – a reasonable yardstick of likely loyalty. Why not start a procedure whereby the chairman automatically sends a personalised word-processed letter to all new shareholders welcoming them and thanking them for their confidence in your company. As for the more influential City press (the *FT*'s Lex column remains far and away the most important), do you have a record of their last personal contact with your company, and what their own cuttings files are likely to throw up if they had to produce a story to a deadline about, say, an unexpected bid for you?

**Employees:** again there are many different sub-groups requiring different types of communication: the board (executive and non-executive directors), production, line and supervisory management, shop-floor workers, administrative and distribution staff, finance, personnel, sales and marketing etc, head office if you are a division.

List how you currently communicate with these various groups:

- team briefings
- works councils
- the noticeboard
- the house journal
- company conferences
- video

■ trade and national advertising

■ employees' and shareholders' annual reports

■ the trade and national press

■ through trade union channels etc.

Estimate which means of communication work best. If different groups were grilled by a researcher, what would they list as the most important sources of information about the company, its products and its progress? The canteen grapevine or the house journal, their supervisors or their shop stewards?

---

You will now have a much clearer idea of how open your organisation is, and what it expects from you. The good news is that the strength of organisational cultures today is less draconian than it used to be.

Here, for example, are the 'Office Staff Practice' rules which were enforced at a counting house in Lichfield back in 1852.

1. Godliness, cleanliness, and punctuality are the necessities of a good business.

2. This firm has reduced the hours of work and the clerical staff will now only have to be present between the hours of 7.00 am and 6.00 pm on weekdays.

3. Daily prayers will be held each morning in the main office. The clerical staff will be present.

4. Clothing must be of a sober nature. The clerical staff will not disport themselves in raiment of bright colours, nor will they wear hose, unless in good repair.

5. Overshoes and top-coats may not be worn in the office, but neckscarves and headwear may be worn in inclement weather.

6. A stove is provided for the benefit of clerical staff; coal and wood must be kept in the locker. It is recommended that each member of the clerical staff bring four pounds of coal each day during cold weather.

7. No member of the clerical staff may leave the room without

permission from Mr Rogers. The calls of nature are permitted, and clerical staff may use the garden below the second gate. This area must be kept in good order.

8.  No talking is allowed during business hours.

9.  The craving of tobacco, wines or spirits is a human weakness, and, as such, is forbidden to all members of the clerical staff.

10. Now that the hours of business have been drastically reduced the partaking of food is allowed between 11.30am and noon, but work will not, on any account, cease.

11. Members of the clerical staff will provide their own pens. A new sharpener is available, on application to Mr Rogers.

12. Mr Rogers will nominate a senior clerk to be responsible for the cleanliness of the main office and the private office, and all boys and juniors will report to him 40 minutes before prayers, and will remain after closing hours for similar work. Brushes, brooms, scrubbers and soap are provided by the owners.

13. The new increased weekly wages are as detailed hereunder:

| | | | |
|---|---|---|---|
| Junior boys | | Boys (to 14 years) | - 2/1d |
| (to 11 years) | - 1/4d | Junior clerks | - 8/7d |
| Juniors | - 4/8d | Senior clerks | |
| Clerks | - 10/9d | (after 15 years | |
| | | with the owners) | - 21/-d |

The owners recognise the generosity of the new Labour Laws, but will expect a great rise in output of work to compensate for these near-Utopian conditions. (*Human Engineering*, Lord Robens, Jonathan Cape, London, 1970.)

Just think, keep your head down and in fifteen years you could get Mr Rogers' job – pen sharpener and all! In fact, then as now, emulating Mr Rogers is the best advice possible, ie bury as much of your maverick, non-conformist personality as you sensibly can. As Francis Bacon wrote, 'anger makes dull men witty, but keeps them poor'.

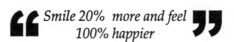

    *Smile 20% more and feel 100% happier*

Happiness and success come from shared values and goals. Transcendentalist Ralph Waldo Emerson, in his book *Representative Men*, captured the spirit of this beautifully:

> If there is love between us, inconceivably delicious and profitable will our intercourse be; if not, your time is lost, and you will only annoy me. I shall seem to you stupid, and the reputation I have false. All my good is magnetic, and I educate not by lessons, but by going about my business.

---

### SPY ON YOURSELF

Some senior managers conduct 'mystery shopper' checks on their own organisations. It's common for directors of major retailers and food chains to visit outlets anonymously to check up. Some bosses ring in to their salespeople or send complaints letters to see the speed and style of response.

It can backfire. A chairman of British Rail once told me that he was leaving the headquarters building late one evening and heard a direct line telephone ringing on someone's desk. He picked it up and an irate passenger demanded to know to whom he was speaking. 'I'm the chairman, how can I help?' was the reply. After a pause the man said, 'Good grief, it's come to this. The chairman answering the switchboard now!'

---

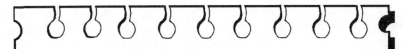

## SUMMARY

Apply *The 20% Factor* and win by a length, not a head:

- Know your organisation
- Improve your product knowledge
- Anticipate customer requirements
- Maintain and improve communications.

# 8 THE ORGANISATION CULTURE

Naturally you will find it easier to understand the culture and dynamics of your own organisation. However, if you are looking for a job with a new company, or having to sell to different companies, you need to know how to interpret *their* needs and values.

Any organisation can be made to seem like an individual, given a little imagination. This is a useful way of helping you to understand other organisations and employers better, and to categorise customers from other, perhaps very different, corporate backgrounds. The corporate cultures, for example, at Unilever, Mars, SmithKline Beecham and Sony are very different, and if you are unable to recognise this and adjust quickly then your dealings with these corporations will be a disappointment.

You can begin to understand an organisation's corporate culture from four main sources:

- its products and brands

- its people (from switchboard operators to senior management)

- its literature

- its buildings.

We will look at each in turn.

## YOU'RE NEVER ALONE WITH A BRAND

If companies and organisations can be enlikened to people, then this is even more true for products, brands, which can be like familiar old friends.

To American GIs in the war, Coke and Pepsi, Lucky Strikes, Hershie Bars and Wrigley's gum were literally a taste of home, the taste of their girlfriend's last kiss at the quayside.

Some brands really do have a personality, characters real or cartoon, who we have got to know through advertising and packaging. Mr Cube, the Homepride Flour Graders, Mr Kipling, the Bisto Kids, Captain Birdseye, the Milky Bar Kid, Oxo Kate, the Ovaltineys, the Milk Tray Man, the Dulux English sheepdog, Arthur the Kattomeat cat, and of course the PG Tips chimpanzees. Other brands link themselves with existing well known people, mainly from the worlds of show business or sport, whose existing public persona fits well with the way the marketers want the brand to be viewed.

After the *Endurance* had been lost, crushed in 1912 by ice in the bleak southern seas, Ernest Shackleton, whilst stranded with his crew on an ice flow 346 miles from the nearest food and shelter, salvaged a number of judicious necessities from the fast disintegrating wreck. The first things he subsequently issued were 'a complete new set of Burberrys and underclothing to each man' and 'ten of the Jaeger woollen [sleeping] bags' – surely some small comfort for all with their familiarity from home; truly life-saving placebos.

And however distant from home I am, in India or East Africa, a British Airways sign still makes me feel that home is not, after all, that far away, and that they would indeed still take more care of me if I needed something. The BBC has the same effect, as do most international hotels – Hiltons, Inter-Continentals – embassies of a kind, all of them, for the lonely disorientated business traveller. We trust great brands.

The Squibb drugs company in the US captured a great truth in its first ever advertising campaign in 1921 – 'The priceless ingredient of every product is the honour and integrity of its maker'. This was just a year before a date on which advertising agency bosses should now bow three times in the direction of their paper millions – 28 August. On that day in 1922, at 1700 hours, the first ever advertisement was broadcast, on a New York radio station.

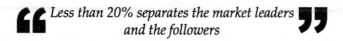

**❝** *Less than 20% separates the market leaders and the followers* **❞**

Leading brands even have their own guardians and protectors within the marketing department – brand managers – whose job it is to promote the brand yet remain the steward of its integrity.

Seemingly strange words to use in this connection with a mere product, but real brands are very much more than just a mere product. A Mars Bar, for example, is something we have all grown up with and in the words of one of the best advertising copy lines ever written, it has helped us 'work, rest and play'. What a marvellous way to present the simple enjoyment of a snack, a chocolate bar. As a consumer, I don't want to see them involved in any kind of nasty promotion, and I don't ever want to see that famous, trusted friend's name and logo cheapened. I don't want that, and you can be sure Mr Mars (yes, there is a Mr Mars) and his marketers feel just the same way. They won't let me down.

Hoover, Guinness, Fairy Liquid, Singer Sewing Machines, Church's shoes, Persil, Heinz Beans, Parker Pens, Pyrex Ovenware, Rolls Royce Motors, HP Sauce, Christy's towels ... I trust all of these brands and confidently expect them to behave and perform in certain ways. Some may be in decline for all I know, and their brand managers worried about their modernity, about their relevance to today, and where they fit into their positioning statement to take them to the late 1990s. But as a consumer, my reaction is extremely conservative. Leave things as they are. Don't tinker with my old friends.

Clearly an intimate understanding of market needs and of brand personality is fundamental. This can be surprisingly detailed, with in-depth analysis of 'shell values' – that is the obvious propositions(s) of the brand (its unique selling points, its taste, price positioning, visual impact, colour, its role as a badge for peer group status etc) – and the 'yolk values', the properties which contribute almost subliminally to the consumers' perception and enjoyment of the brand (its heritage, its inner strengths, its reassurance values as a kind of placebo etc). Good brand managers can probably tell you more about their brand than about their spouse, and will certainly remember the dates when Nielsen or AGB research data on their sales and market share are due more easily than family anniversaries and birthdays.

**"** *A 20% giveaway is one of the most successful sales promotion techniques* **"**

## MOTIVATING PEOPLE

It is joked that dog owners eventually come to resemble their pets. Most certainly employees do come to reflect the values and style of their organisation.

You should learn to recognise the collegiate or bridge to engine room company, and the differing natures of entrepreneurs and salaried managers. We have already analysed how closely your own perceived character fits with that of your company.

A useful way of bringing a degree of science into generalising on how the people in an organisation reflect its values is to study Abraham Maslow. In his book *Motivation and Personality* (Harper & Brother, New York, 1954) Maslow, a humanist psychologist, looked at a person's hierarchy of needs. He argued that once basic needs – food, shelter, warmth, safety etc – are satisfied, then a person's attention turns to 'higher-order needs'.

The triangle chart of Maslow's Hierarchy of Needs (Alderfer's Classification) shows this progression.

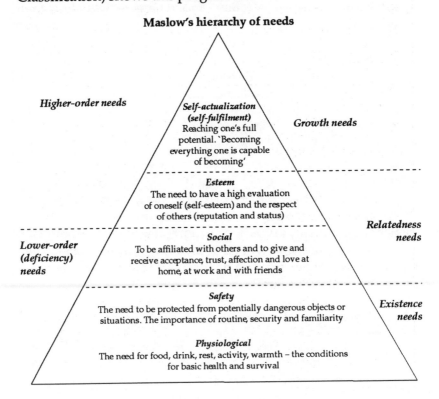

**Maslow's hierarchy of needs**

*Higher-order needs*

*Self-actualization (self-fulfilment)*
Reaching one's full potential. 'Becoming everything one is capable of becoming'

*Growth needs*

*Esteem*
The need to have a high evaluation of oneself (self-esteem) and the respect of others (reputation and status)

*Relatedness needs*

*Lower-order (deficiency) needs*

*Social*
To be affiliated with others and to give and receive acceptance, trust, affection and love at home, at work and with friends

*Safety*
The need to be protected from potentially dangerous objects or situations. The importance of routine, security and familiarity

*Existence needs*

*Physiological*
The need for food, drink, rest, activity, warmth – the conditions for basic health and survival

My own view is that although Maslow's 'lower order existence needs' were meant to relate to having a hearth and home to keep the wolf from the door, the bullying tactics of some companies and the fear they engender – fear of redundancy or public humiliation – reduce some individuals to the bottom of the triangle in their business life.

On the other hand, in excellent companies you see evidence of individuals blossoming right up to the top – giving irrational loyalty and long hours to that company, taking on more and more unpaid responsibilities. I see it in companies where senior management 'walks the job' regularly and says 'well done' regularly.

### HOW TO DISCIPLINE PEOPLE

You can't always say 'well done' of course. If you do have to warn and discipline people, here are some tips on how to accomplish it leaving your dignity and theirs in tact.

■ Ensure you have in the first place very clearly communicated what you consider unacceptable behaviour or attitudes.

■ Reassure yourself that there is group acceptance to these standards.

■ Make it clear that punishment for breaches is inevitable.

■ Never threaten action on which you cannot deliver for physical, legal or trade union reasons.

■ Other than for gross breaches of discipline, always give warnings and put them in writing.

■ Establish why any breach has occurred: the reason may colour your own or the group view of what punishment, if any, is merited. It may leave the transgressor with some dignity.

■ Remain calm and formal – not angry or informal. You are the instrument of accepted codes. Don't let them see if you feel cross or let down. Distance yourself, remain impersonal. It will help you and them redevelop a positive relationship later.

■ Make punishments neither too harsh nor too lenient. Don't seem vindictive or 'throw the book' at them. Equally don't apologise for handing out the punishment. It should seem a natural consequence of their own behaviour – not of yours.

■ Consider having somebody with you when giving warnings and when disciplining. As management consultant Vincent Nolan has said, when dealing with conflict, 90 per cent of the emotion is about 10 per cent of the content. People can become irrational and their memories blank or highly selective. They can also make malicious complaints about you unless there is a witness.

It is the regular person – not the ambitious winners – who most value this recognition. They know they are not shooting stars in the organisation, either through choice or through limited ability, but they do believe themselves to be diligent, reliable and the people who make any enterprise actually work. Clerical workers, cleaners, post room people, copy typists, telephonists, messengers, security men – they *are* the company in many respects.

In too many organisations recognition of ordinary folk only comes with retirement, or when they leave to take up another job or have a baby. If management spent as much time praising good work on a routine basis as they do thinking up things to say in leaving party speeches, then so much more would be achieved.

One sign of a responsive, motivated organisation is when people start talking face to face or on the telephone about problems, instead of sending memos, copied around the place.

---

### TEAM SPIRIT

The chairman of a big holiday company told me of the high morale in his complaints section – a tough and stressful department. The head of the unit was away for a couple of weeks and her in-tray had been steadily growing – a miserable sight to see on return from holiday. One of her clerks noticed this, put a pack of Polo mints on the table and said 'Right. Whoever clears the biggest number of her files gets the mints.' Everyone joined in to clear the backlog, and the 'winner' shared the mints with everyone else. No need there for big sticks or big incentives.

---

The point is that in a successful organisation everyone who contributes to that success on a regular, on-going even routine basis is part of a winning team, and by definition a winner themselves. It is not just the chief executive, the supersalesman or the boffin who put the stripe in the toothpaste who are the winners – the whole organisation is the real winner. A regular supporter of a winning football team feels like a winner too, just as much as, and sometimes *more* than the career professionals on the pitch and on the bench. A manager or captain who thanks his supporters in the programme, on a TV interview or over the public address system, is being very shrewd.

If most people are winners in this context, the managers who realise it, walk the floor and acknowledge it, can achieve dramatic and lasting benefits. Effective and popular leaders put into practice this principle. So do good schoolteachers, sports coaches and good parents. Praise and encouragement have also been proven to be important tools in the treatment of children and others with psychological problems, as well as in the rehabilitation of offenders.

The northern European suspicion of anything other than the big stick – or at least the stick and carrot – approach to motivation, however, still leaves many managers, parents and teachers uncomfortable about using too much praise. It is seen as soft or weak. The reality is that the corollary of a management style which is based on encouragement and praise is the very tough expectations it raises amongst bosses and workmates, peer groups, for consistent good work, self-discipline and to not let the side down in any way. Self-policing can be the toughest form of policing of all – there can be no fun in getting away with things, you *know* what makes up a good day's work, and so do those around you. No amount of coming in late, petty pilfering, malicious gossip and bad-mouthing the company is acceptable. You're treated as important, as a winner – and only losers and nobodies behave that way, don't they?

## Saying thank you

This awareness of the importance of others can be carried over profitably into business and social life outside a work environment. Acknowledging the role and importance of others becomes a way of life which can make your own life so much more pleasant and less stressful. If when your barber asks how you want your hair cut you snap back, 'in silence', then don't expect a great haircut. If you don't make any effort with eye contact, body language and common courtesy with shop assistants, bus conductors or bank clerks, then chances are you will be shaving off a little of the joy that can be found in life from others.

As you can see, it is not true that it costs nothing to say 'thank you'. It costs time and it costs in terms of analysing your nature and recasting it a little if necessary. If by temperament you are more of a loner than a team manager, short-tempered and self-centred, then saying 'thank you' as if you mean it, in a non-contrived 'this is me saying thank you' kind of way, certainly will cost. But the effort is self-evidently worth it.

## None so deaf ...

... as those who will not hear.

Another common obstacle to communication and business success is the inability of people in authority to listen, and as a result the inability of the enterprise to react to things that customers, the market and its own people are saying.

The Greeks believed that ideally a town should grow no larger than the size of crowd that can hear the voice of one man. There remains a great deal of truth in this because even though we now have microphones, loudspeakers, written media, films, TV, radio and videos, we still miss the point. We have certainly grown into far larger groups that can still hear the voice of one person – but have we yet developed any interactive way permitting us to question that person? That was the point, and it remains just as valid today despite all our smart technology. It need not be a problem in companies, however. Most group sizes permit dialogue – listening as well as speaking.

The problem is that most of us don't *want* to listen, and the people with whom we think we communicate don't either. Add to this the fact that we only retain about ten per cent of what we are told anyway, and only understand less than ten per cent of the words in the English language, and the scale of the listening problem becomes clear.

Some knowledge of the psychological barriers can help us towards an understanding of our own shortcomings, and through that to those of others and how to cope with them and their organisations.

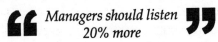

**Managers should listen 20% more**

The suggestion that we should listen to someone in a work environment may well be met with resistance because we tend to feel most comfortable with a status quo. We are all generally suspicious and resistant to change which new information may herald. Also, if we have a shrewd idea that the topic of the communication is something we feel strongly about, then there is even less likelihood of our agreeing to listen to arguments or counter-arguments. After all, it is a subject upon which we have already deliberated and reached a public or private conclusion which satisfies us.

The chances are we will not listen, but anticipate what is being said and go on to a kind of mental auto-pilot, nodding and 'humphing' until we can butt in and give our own views. It is probable that this unwelcome interruption will not be listened to either, and the other party will simply bide time waiting for a cue to grab the conversation back, at which point we switch off, go back onto auto-pilot, and so on. We can all think of subjects on which we admittedly have closed minds.

I am implacably opposed to the reintroduction of hanging, and no amount of persuasion, facts and figures are likely to sway me. It's rather like discussing politics or religion with committed people.

If we find our views being challenged, or worse still feel we are being criticised in some implied or explicit way, then we have more than boredom to cope with. Frustration may arise, characterised by aggression, regression, fixation and resignation – all states capable of being experimentally induced in clinical conditions. All of this will certainly make effective communication near impossible. Aggression, apart from the obvious risk of physical attack, can include throwing things, verbal abuse, slamming doors, kicking wastebins, or self-inflicted injuries like punching the wall. Regression can lead to juvenile behaviour – crying, telling tales, sulking and pouting perhaps, going back to childhood escapes which may then have worked.

## Fixation

Fixation is where the person cannot concentrate on the subject under review and instead some act or gesture is repeated again and again, even though he or she knows it will achieve little – Lady Macbeth washing her hands time and time again to get rid of imagined blood stains is a good example of a fixation. Pipe-smokers may scrape their pipe-bowl noisily with a penknife, others may persistently smooth their hair back.

It was alleged that millionaire Howard Hughes became obsessed with the need to avoid germs and diseases. Even more serious can be the state of 'resignation' sometimes found amongst the homeless or the unemployed, people who have simply given up. A typical resigned response in a commercial situation might be: 'I've put up with this place for twenty years, nothing will ever change'. People in this state of mind spread depression and will no longer try to make things better.

Try and spot any of these traits in yourself and others around you. Employees in these states of mind can become highly susceptible to being led and organised by other malcontents. If things get really bad the better people and customers of course simply go elsewhere, if they can. If situations do reach an extreme, then it is wise to create a set of circumstances for yourself or for others in which people can express their frustration without subsequent embarrassment or criticism.

Criticism never really works because we either do not accept that we are in the wrong at all, or resent having our noses rubbed in our more obvious mistakes. Let them blow off steam. This is known as *catharsis* and is a basic form of therapy. Talking to a trained counsellor or company friend, or writing down your annoyances, can make you feel so much better, and help you put things into perspective. Some American companies hold 'rap sessions', where management or supervisors make themselves available to employees who can sound off about things if they want to, and generally tell them how things ought to be run.

## Morale

The real solution is to create the kind of environment in which morale is high, people are interested and committed, and in which regular short, factual, two-way communication is expected and welcome.

If bosses won't listen, if the board seems deaf to new ideas, then it can often help to have respected outside third parties make the case for you – perhaps a leading management consultancy firm, a market research de-brief by the agency, or even one or two customers friendly to you passing remarks. Then it can become *their* idea, *their* views, not just a reluctant acceptance of something from a subordinate which, by implication, they should have realised themselves. A window on the outside world may be necessary to cast fresh light.

Top management is subject to frustration, even to the point of regression, as much as anybody and more than most. Symptoms include difficulty in making apparently routine judgements, reluctance to delegate, becoming very thin-skinned, and developing irrational fixations with routine trivia, like expenses sheets or bad timekeeping. Meanwhile the strategic issues go unaddressed, they begin to speak in broad generalisations without relating them to specific issues where decisions are required, and they develop irrational support for certain people and points of view. The loss of judgement and inability to make distinctions obvious to others is one sign that they may have regressed. Another is uncritical suggestibility. So is a longing to return to the familiar past as a place of refuge, accompanied by an unwillingness to face the future, change. The 'good old days' and previous, now-retired or deceased managers and directors can be elevated to rose-tinted perfection, their likes and qualities never to be met again.

The relief from whatever pressures are causing the problems is the rather obvious best solution, if they are known and actionable. If not, catharsis with the help of his or her immediate peer group – a problem aired and shared – should help, as would counselling and role-playing if circumstances could be created to make them accessible, perhaps on a suitable residential senior management course.

Should you really believe your boss to be in such a state of regression as to need psychiatric help, telling him would not be a wise career move! And remember that our own reactions to people suffering from different levels of frustration may not be entirely rational either. We may become hostile and so make the situation even worse. The temptation is to misjudge their symptoms and treat the people as useless and awkward. Quite a vicious circle.

The next time you find yourself getting steamed up about something, consider whether your judgement has become irrational because of frustration: consider the possibility that you might after all be wrong. Blaming others, the creation of scapegoats is a classic and dangerous feature of frustration. At one extreme, a study reported in the USA in 1940 showed a strong correlation between the number of people lynched – negroes mainly – and the price of cotton (Minor [sic] Studies in Aggression: VI Correlations of Lynchings with Economic Indices' by C I Hovland and R R Sears, the *Journal of Psychology*). In a more general sense blaming the boss, blaming assistants, blaming production, blaming component suppliers ... is a good telltale warning to ourselves to stand back and reassess whether that is the real truth. Again, we must work to know ourselves.

## PROJECTING A POSITIVE CORPORATE IMAGE

### Corporate literature

Another good way to obtain clues about a corporation's culture and style is by studying its corporate literature. Letterheads, logos, business cards, brochures, annual reports, company newspapers, vans and lorry livery and the layout, language and design of recruitment advertisements – all can give you valuable information.

An organisation which has recently had its corporate identity and logo redesigned probably thought its image was previously dull or old fashioned, and lagging behind where it believes itself to be. One with old fashioned, out of date logos is probably being led by a chief executive who has been in the job a very long time, and may be the founder – someone who doesn't like change, nor wants to be seen 'wasting' shareholders' money on jazzy design agency fees.

A company with a chief executive whose photograph appears on every page of the house newspaper, and dominates the annual report at the expense of fellow directors, may well be one in which sycophancy and blandishment are as important to getting on as competence.

### Confidence building

The culture and tone of voice of an organisation, as we have seen, is one important clue to its personality. Its 'dress sense' – architecture and interior design – is another.

There are many stereotypes of how we expect certain types of office/business building and interiors to look – banks a little dark with mahogany doors, the manager behind a green leather-topped desk; advertising agencies, all glass, chrome, open-plan and potted palms; an engineering company, flat-roofed, low-rise 1950s, with pictures of dour founders on the wall, apprentice-boy pieces in glass cases, and a pervading smell of hot oil wafting in from somewhere – and so on.

The choice of office building in which organisations receive visitors says a lot about them. The use of architecture and design in this way of course is not new, and over history it has been taken to some extraordinary lengths – such as at Versailles.

In ancient China in the thirteenth century Kublai Khan had quite a family to feed, and many subjects and visitors to impress. He had four wives, each with their own court of over 300 damsels, plus pages, eunuchs and other attendants amounting to more than 10,000 persons per wife. Venetian trader Marco Polo, then twenty-one, and by any other name one of Khan's key account customers, was clearly impressed by his Imperial supplier when he wrote of the awesome spectacle of the Hall of the Palace, an area which could easily dine 6000 people. 'The building is altogether so vast, so rich and so beautiful, that no man on earth could design anything superior to it. The outside of the roof also is all colours with vermilion and yellow and green and blue and other hues, which are fixed with a varnish so fine and exquisite that they shine like crystal, and lend a resplendent lustre to the Palace as seen for a great way round.'

Architecture through the ages has generally had a clear objective in mind – commercial, political or religious. Renaissance Florence was shaped by successful merchants like the Medici; Napoleon and Haussmann for their differing reasons left their mark on Paris; Empress Maria-Theresa and Franz-Joseph on Vienna; Mussolini on Rome. The church of course is the real master in the use of architecture and design to meet objectives. Visit Sacré Coeur in Paris, having imagined the surrounding poor neighbourhoods a century or more ago. Then, pretend you are a local Parisian of the eighteenth or nineteenth century living in a candlelit hovel, and look up at the huge figure of Christ in the dome – eyes staring straight at you, arms ready to embrace you. As for St Peter's...

Business architecture has changed dramatically in recent years, however. Look at the Victorian bank buildings, or more particularly at the pension and assurance buildings in the major cities of London, Manchester, Newcastle, Glasgow, and the rest. They look like great cathedralesque edifices that may not have pleased Lord Clark's eye, but would have told him something about their confidence and civilisation. It is clear that the brief for the Victorian architects was to create buildings which would reassure ordinary people, first, that if their money was inside it was impregnably guarded, and secondly, that these organisations taking your shillings and pence for retirement pensions and rainy days would actually be around when you came to collect it. They were literally built to last. The *Building Chronicle* in the mid-nineteenth century remarked that classical architecture suited banks, since it denoted 'a sentiment of enduring strength and close security, a manner which may signify a solid and confident substantiality'.

The needs of the market are now very different. People do not need reassuring that the banks and pension companies have got their money safely locked away, nor that they are going to be around in fifty years. That is taken for granted. What customers now expect is for their financial institutions to be modern, high-tech, on the ball and bustling with bright young people and computers.

The dramatic changes in retailing are obvious enough. Self-service supermarkets with highly computerised price coding and stock control, open-plan banks and building societies, and round-the-clock automatic teller machines. Petrol stations where we service ourselves, and even armchair shopping using viewdata.

It is not the companies that have changed, it is the customer who has revised his or her expectations from suppliers. The view of what is good service has changed dramatically. Good service for most now increasingly means minimal human contact and fast service.

---

### NOT TOO SHOWY

If all this has given you a taste for brightening up the directors' dining room, then I suggest you stop short at emulating the next two observations by Marco Polo, for fear of giving your MD ideas above his station:

At every door of the hall (or, indeed, wherever the Emperor may be) there stand a couple of big men like giants, one on each side, armed with staves. Their business is to see that no one steps upon the threshold in entering, and if this does happen, they strip the offender of his clothes, and he must pay a forfeit to have them back again; or in lieu of taking his clothes, they give him a certain number of blows . . .

They have the mouth and nose muffled with fine napkins of silk and gold, so that no breath nor odour from their persons should taint the dish or the goblet presented to the Lord. And when he takes the cup all the Barons and the rest of the company drop on their knees and make the deepest obeisance before him, and then the Emperor doth drink. But each time that he does so the whole ceremony is repeated . . .

Overall then, whereas conservatism in dress for individuals still remains sound advice, there are very few businesses for which modernity is now inappropriate in terms of offices – safe modernity, that is, with no evidence of conspicuous spending on original Hockneys or Moores.

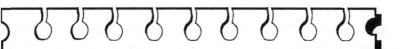

## SUMMARY

The essence of *The 20% Factor* is to anticipate and meet needs – both yours and those of your customers, so:

- Keep in touch!

- Clue up on corporate culture

- Anticipate employer and customer requirements.

# 9 WHAT KIND OF MANAGER ARE YOU?

Once you have become skilled in recognising a company's culture you will be able to adopt the management style that is most likely to lead to promotion and success. Use *The 20% Factor* to package yourself accordingly.

In some companies the management style may be very open, participative and collegiate. This kind of organisation may have briefing group systems for cascading information down, and to help engender team involvement in, and hence acceptance of, decisions being taken. It may have quality circles and it may see different departments and job functions as 'internal customers', to be treated in the same way as regular customers. This type of company may have put its employees through customer orientation training, and be wedded to regular house newspapers and perhaps videos to keep everyone informed and motivated. Look for these signs.

> **"** *Team briefing should take up 20% of your time* **"**

At the other extreme from the open communicating organisation we have the 'bridge to engine room' style of autocratic management, where you do what you're told, and are not expected to question it – rather like our Lichfield counting house. This style is often seen in companies where there is a founder, or a strong family dynasty, reflecting the entrepreneurial aggression and single-mindedness that is behind most successful business start-ups. Unless you have had your home on the line as bank security for your company, it is hard to understand why these people behave this way.

Let's try and analyse the kind of management styles that you are currently most comfortable with, and then you can judge whether this is compatible with your own organisation's prevailing style. Discover whether you are a ruthless Machiavellian or perhaps a shallow Starquest type desperate for applause and glory, whether you are a teamplayer or loner. Complete the management style assessment and the team work analysis now.

## Discover your management styles

Complete this assessment by noting the response which best reflects your feelings about the statements. Ring your responses to each of the thirty questions or — if you really must — list them *alongside the question number* on a separate sheet of paper (you are going to have to do more than simply add up all the a, b, c and ds). It is important to answer honestly in order to gain an accurate insight into your real approach to business.

1. I am skilled at getting my own way.

   a Very true
   b True much of the time
   c Occasionally true
   d Hardly true at all.

2. I achieve my goals in life.

   a Very true
   b True much of the time
   c Occasionally true
   d Hardly ever true.

3. I demand recognition for my accomplishments.

   a Very true
   b True much of the time
   c Occasionally true
   d Not true at all.

4. I pride myself on offering moral leadership.

   a Very true
   b True much of the time
   c Occasionally true
   d Not true at all.

5. I believe most problems in life are best left to solve themselves.

*a* Very true
*b* True much of the time
*c* Occasionally true
*d* Not true at all.

6. I face the future with great optimism.

*a* Very true
*b* True much of the time
*c* Occasionally true
*d* Not true at all.

7. I take advantage of other people's weaknesses.

*a* Very true
*b* True much of the time
*c* Occasionally true
*d* Not true at all.

8. I manipulate situations to suit my own purposes.

*a* Very true
*b* True much of the time
*c* Occasionally true
*d* Not true at all.

9. I offer sound advice.

*a* Very true
*b* True much of the time
*c* Occasionally true
*d* Hardly ever true.

10. I set myself tough challenges in life.

*a* Very true
*b* True much of the time
*c* Occasionally true
*d* Not true at all.

11. I believe most people have a lot of good in them.

*a* Very true
*b* True much of the time

    *c* Occasionally true
    *d* Not true at all.

12.  I am cautious about adopting new ideas.

    *a* Very true
    *b* True much of the time
    *c* Occasionally true
    *d* Not true at all.

13.  I get a thrill out of being in the public eye.

    *a* Very true
    *b* True much of the time
    *c* Occasionally true
    *d* Not true at all.

14.  I am an excellent judge of people.

    *a* Very true
    *b* True much of the time
    *c* Occasionally true
    *d* Not true at all.

15.  I will be ruthless, if necessary, to achieve my goals in life.

    *a* Very true
    *b* True much of the time
    *c* Occasionally true
    *d* Not true at all.

16.  I trust my colleagues absolutely.

    *a* Very true
    *b* True to a considerable extent
    *c* True to some extent
    *d* Not true at all.

17.  I make detailed plans for the future.

    *a* Very true
    *b* True to a considerable extent
    *c* True to some extent
    *d* Not true at all.

18. I love being in front of an audience.

    *a* Very true
    *b* True to a considerable extent
    *c* True to some extent
    *d* Not true at all.

19. I take pride in working longer hours than most of my colleagues.

    *a* Very true
    *b* True much of the time
    *c* Occasionally true
    *d* Not true at all.

20. I am wise in the ways of the world.

    *a* Very true
    *b* True to a considerable extent
    *c* True to some extent
    *d* Not true at all.

21. I like to know everything that goes on at work.

    *a* Very true
    *b* True much of the time
    *c* Occasionally true
    *d* Hardly ever true.

22. I avoid taking risks.

    *a* Very true
    *b* True much of the time
    *c* Occasionally true
    *d* Hardly ever true.

23. I am reluctant to introduce changes at work.

    *a* Very true
    *b* True to a considerable extent
    *c* True to some extent
    *d* Not true at all.

24. I don't like to think about my failures.

    *a* Very true
    *b* True much of the time

*c* Occasionally true
*d* Hardly ever true.

25. I seek ways of making myself more popular.

    *a* Very true
    *b* True much of the time
    *c* Occasionally true
    *d* Hardly ever true.

26. I am always ready to offer advice.

    *a* Very true
    *b* True much of the time
    *c* Occasionally true
    *d* Hardly ever true.

27. I thrive on hard work.

    *a* Very true
    *b* True much of the time
    *c* Occasionally true
    *d* Hardly ever true.

28. I constantly strive for perfection.

    *a* Very true
    *b* True much of the time
    *c* Occasionally true
    *d* Not true at all.

29. I believe every cloud has a silver lining.

    *a* Very true
    *b* True much of the time
    *c* Occasionally true
    *d* Hardly ever true.

30. I have a very charismatic personality.

    *a* Very true
    *b* True much of the time
    *c* Occasionally true
    *d* Not true at all.

## How to score

The assessment has explored six management styles. Score by awarding four points for each a response, two for b, one for c and zero for d, according to the table below. For example, if your answer to question one was b, write b alongside the Machiavelli line under 'Your scores'. If your answer to question two was a, write a alongside the Superman line, and so on. Then add up the score for each 'Management style' line and enter it under 'Totals'.

| Management style | Statements | Your scores | Totals |
| --- | --- | --- | --- |
| Machiavelli | 1; 7; 8; 15; 21 | | |
| Panglossian | 6; 11; 16; 24; 29 | | |
| Superman | 2; 10; 19; 27; 28 | | |
| Starquest | 3; 13; 18; 25; 30 | | |
| Noah | 5; 12; 17; 22; 23 | | |
| Guru | 4; 9; 14; 20; 26 | | |

To see how these styles relate to one another and the extent to which they may prove a help or a handicap in your career, fill in your scores on the table on page 122 by drawing them in as a bar chart. Simply rule off each score in the six columns and sketch in some diagonal lines under each line to fill it in.

## What your scores reveal

The highest score represents your primary management style, the second highest your next most frequently adopted approach. Similar scores on two or more styles means you are able to switch between them according to circumstances.

Ideally all the qualities explored by this assessment, and described below, should be present for effective management and should rate around ten. However, if any of the scores is higher than ten, there is a real risk of it dominating your strategic thinking to the point where it becomes inflexible and far less effective. Scores below ten, however, suggest that the style is used too infrequently, so reducing your effectiveness in many situations. The higher or lower the score the less successfully you are employing that particular style.

Practise using those on which your score was low, and try to reduce the frequency of high-scoring approaches.

## What the styles involve

**Machiavelli** was the celebrated Florentine statesman and author of *The Prince,* a classic account of ruthless statecraft.

As a result his name has long been synonymous with intrigue and low cunning. In moderation this can be a valuable management skill, allowing you to out think and out manoeuvre the opposition. It can help you pre-empt the intrigues of others, and proves an invaluable survival skill at times of boardroom coups. When the game is hard, fast and dirty, the competition tough and no prisoners are being taken, a Machiavelli style really comes into its own. Taken to extremes, however, it poisons the atmosphere by breeding widespread mistrust and undermining morale.

**Pangloss** was a character in Voltaire's *Candide* renowned for his incurable and misleading optimism. Despite the misfortunes it brought him, he believed to the end that 'all is for the best in this best of all possible worlds'. While it's always better to look on the bright side than to wallow in every misfortune, excessive optimism is as ineffective a management style as complete pessimism. A balance must be struck in order to confront problems objectively, and anticipate when, where and why things may go awry.

**Superman**: there needs to be more than a touch of superman in every successful executive. If you don't have great faith in your abilities, who else will? But some executives get so carried away by a belief in their superhuman abilities they mistrust any judgement but their own, refuse to delegate and are prime candidates for coronary heart disease. Overdoing the macho approach risks destroying all you have strived so hard to create.

**Starquest**: when this style dominates there is a constant desire to win the admiration, approval and – above all – the attention of others.

Playing to the gallery and yearning for applause means that decisions are too often influenced by the glory they are likely to attract, instead of sound management practice. Those who always need to be centre stage are hard to work for and almost impossible to work with. While it's important to ensure one's accomplishments are noticed, this doesn't mean constantly stealing the limelight. The place for stars is show business, not big business.

**Noah**: he paid attention to warnings from a reliable source, prudently built his ark and so weathered a storm. And it's true that the ark was built by amateurs and the *Titanic* by professionals. There are certainly times when Noah's cautious, DIY play-safe style is no more than sound common sense and good business practice. But, these days, running for shelter whenever economic storms are threatened or the going gets rough means you spend more time battening down the hatches than building up the business.

Some managers are so concerned never to get their feet wet that every decision is influenced by fears of a flood which never arrives. While a certain amount of prudence is essential, when taken to extremes it lands you high and dry in a desert of missed chances, and lost opportunities.

**Guru**: a high score here suggests you may too often set yourself up as the office guru or know-all. If so, beware, because outside your special area of expertise your views may be no better than those of anybody else – and are almost certainly inferior to those with specialist training in their field. Guru style can be a spin-off from the superman syndrome, the conviction that the possession of superior wisdom and knowledge entitles one to give advice and pass judgement on every issue. Insisting always that others hear, or worse yet, act on your generalised non-specialist views not only creates justifiable resentment, but also increases the risk of major errors.

---

## Analyse your teamwork

Effective teamwork means balancing decision-making styles. This assessment will allow you to identify your own style, and discover its strengths and weaknesses. Answer the following questions by selecting your most likely response to the situation described.

1. You are given three hot tips at the race track once more. The first two romp home and you win £1000. Will you ...

   a Risk all you've won on the last horse tipped, which is running at odds of 10:1?

   b Decide your luck can't hold out any longer and go home with your winnings?

   c Put half your winnings on the last horse, so that you won't go home empty-handed if it does let you down?

2. You have to move quickly to another part of the country and put your house on the market. The following day you receive a cash

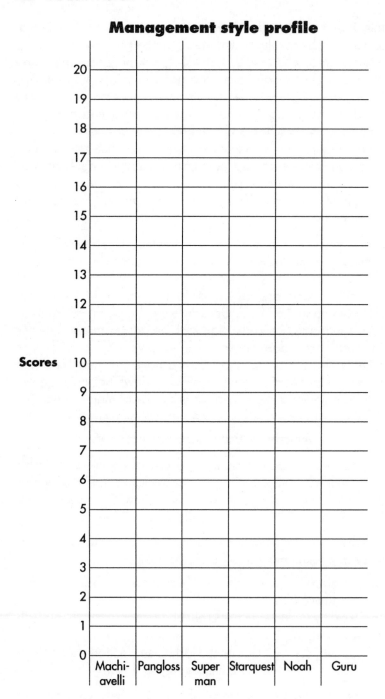

**Management style profile**

offer, but at £5000 less than your asking price. The purchaser insists that this is his top price.

The offer is well below your property's true value and acceptance will put you out of pocket on the new purchase. But you also know there is a serious downturn in house sales in your part of the country and properties similar in price and features to your own are unsold after more than a year. if this happens to you the interest on a large bridging loan will amount to more than you will lose by taking the first offer. Will you ...

a Turn the offer down flat in the hope of getting your asking price?
b Accept rather than lose a rapid sale?
c Stall for as long as possible to keep the prospective purchaser interested while you seek a better offer?

3. You were foolish enough to lend a friend £5000. Now he says his business has failed, he has few assets and cannot repay the loan. But he makes you an offer. He will either give you his last remaining cash, amounting to £2500, or offer a wager on the toss of a coin.

   If he wins you cancel the debt. If he loses, his wife has agreed to part with a family heirloom, a diamond necklace worth £10,000. Do you ...

   a Take the bet because you stand a 50/50 chance of doubling your money?
   b Settle for the £2500?
   c Reject both proposals and insist he find another way of settling his debt in full?

4. While on a business trip abroad you contract a painful and distressing but non-fatal virus. The doctors you consult say there is no cure. Then you find one who has supplies of an experimental drug. He warns that while it has cured similar cases there have also been some fatalities which might have been due to the drug, although this has not been proved. He has only a small amount left, no chance of getting any more and another patient in similar circumstances may claim it before you. Do you ...

   a Agree to the treatment immediately so as not to miss what might be your only chance of a cure?

   *b* Turn it down and continue to search for a safe cure?

   *c* Risk a 48 hour delay before making your decision, so as to try and obtain a second opinion about the risks involved?

5.  You have decided to invest some of your hard-earned savings on the stock market. Three companies are of interest to you.

    The first is a solid but unexciting blue chip stock that will return a steady dividend but never make your fortune.

    The second is a small mining company which, you have heard a whisper, is about to announce a big strike. If true their stocks will soar and you'll reap big rewards. If false their shares will probably prove worthless.

    Finally there is a manufacturing firm which, it is rumoured, will soon be taken over. Should the take-over occur you'll have made an excellent investment. But even without any change it should return a modest profit, but one less than the blue chip company. Are you most likely to ...

   *a* Take a big gamble with the mining company?

   *b* Play safe with a blue chip investment?

   *c* Decide on shares in the manufacturing firm?

6.  Your son is about to start studying law at a prestige university. The trouble is he is far more interested in music than a legal career. He has played lead guitar in an amateur group for many years and musician friends assure you he is very gifted, and the group extremely talented. A week before his studies are due to begin, the group get the offer of an American tour.

    If he accepts it could be the first step to wealth and fame, but he'll lose his place at law school. If he turns down the offer the group will lose what might be the chance of a lifetime. He asks your advice. Do you ...

   *a* Tell him to take the chance in music, after all there are other law schools if the group flops?

   *b* Urge him to forget the tour and not lose the opportunity of obtaining such a prestigious degree?

   *c* Suggest that he try to obtain a deferment from the law school so that he can go on the tour without risking his place?

7.  An American business associate dines at your house and admires a bronze statue in the lounge. You paid £5 for it in a junk shop and loathe it. He says it would be perfect for his home in Texas and offers £500 in cash. You suspect that, while his

liking for the bronze could be genuine, he might also know that it is worth far more. Do you ...

    *a* Refuse his offer on the chance that you'll make more by selling at auction?

    *b* Accept since you'll have made an excellent profit on something you dislike and may not even be worth £500?

    *c* Insist on a valuation before agreeing, even though this could put the sale at risk?

To score this assessment simply total up the number of as, bs and cs selected.

## Majority of as

This is the decision-making style of a *maximiser*. You are willing to take big risks in the hope of maximum rewards. You approach challenges with optimism and confidence, always certain you'll come out on top.

*Strengths*: Sensitivity to the positive aspects of any course of action means that opportunities not obvious to less optimistic decision-makers will be quickly seen. This style typifies the entrepreneur. Teams need somebody who can think big and not shy away from risks.

*Weaknesses*: The willingness to 'go for broke' on every occasion means big wins can be wiped out by equally spectacular losses.

Maximisers on teams need to be balanced by the far more cautious approach of those with a majority of bs.

## Majority of bs

This indicates a *minimising* decision-making style. You always seek to minimise losses should, as you pessimistically predict, things go badly wrong.

*Strengths*: This style is ideally suited to situations entailing a high risk of material loss, whether money or goods. Minimisers are excellent at managing other people's finances because they are unlikely to take risks on speculative proposals, however tempting.

*Weaknesses*: Excessive caution may lead to lost opportunities and missed chances. A team dominated by minimisers will seldom make a mistake – or anything else.

The exact opposite of the maximiser approach, conflict can arise in a team where these two are opposed. But from such a clash can come sound decisions in which neither lose out on opportunities nor involve the company in excessive risks.

## Majority of cs

This is the style of a *minimaxer* whose decisions are strongly influenced by the desire to both minimise their maximum potential loss and maximise their minimum expected gain in any situation.

*Strengths:* Unlike the maximiser who sees only the chance for a big success or the minimiser who emphasises the risks of disaster, the minimaxer pursues a middle course. He, or she, is very aware of discrepancies between what was actually achieved and what might have been accomplished. Minimaxers are irritated by lost chances and powerfully desire to prevent later regrets.

It is a style that comes into its own whenever a team is faced with having to take a decision without knowing enough about the situation.

*Weaknesses:* Because the minimaxer tends to favour a compromise between two extremes, he, or she, is as unlikely to enjoy spectacular coups as to experience catastrophic failures.

If you scored near equal totals on all three letters then you have a very flexible decision-making style and can adapt well to different situations.

To be successful, a team should combine all three styles in equal amounts under a strong but empathic and objective chairperson, who keeps lines of communications open between all team members and has the courage to support both the risk taking of the maximiser and the caution of the minimiser as the situation requires.

---

## TEAMPLAYER OR LONER?

Most of us are teamplayers in terms of management style, and that's exactly what the vast majority of organisations want us to be.

It's important, however, to define 'team'. Some organisations are run on the concept of unit or departmentalised teamwork, others on overall corporate teamwork. Very often the unit/ departmental culture differs subtly from the overall corporate culture which the directors fondly believe permeates the whole. You must know whether, in your organisation, your own performance is being measured against the corporate culture, or against the

---

### THE DUNKIRK SPIRIT

There remains a fond belief that when people have their backs to the wall they all pull together. Just like Dunkirk.

Don't bank on it. Days lost through strikes in the years 1941–1945 in the UK were higher than in 1938, the year before the war. 1944 was the worst – with more days lost than in any year since 1932. Strikes were about the usual peacetime things, mainly wages. This was despite the fact that by spring 1944 wage rates had on average risen by around 11 per cent more than the cost of living – and average earnings by still more due to overtime payments.

The strategically vital coal industry was responsible for two-thirds of days lost in 1944: 1·2 million man days and two million tons of coal were lost in the first quarter of 1944 alone. Minister of Labour, Ernest Bevin, said that action by miners in the Sheffield area had inflicted more damage to the country's industry than a heavy air raid.

(Information compiled by Correlli Barnett, author of *The Audit of War*, Macmillan, London, 1986).

---

departmental group culture. In essence, you must know at every point in your career who precisely your immediate boss is, relative to promotion, and also who your next boss might be.

You cannot do this theoretically; it has to be done relative to real life situations. You need to construct a personal performance review system to analyse your real job and the tasks that make it up, and to ensure you know who you are having to impress.

---

## Personal Performance Review System

The ability effectively to manage the performance of others of course has as a prerequisite the need for you, the manager, to be able to manage your own tasks well. And this can still be done by individual managers in organisations where overall the company culture remains in the communications dark ages.

I would suggest that you tailor-make your own version of the following ten-point personal performance review system.

1. Define, redefine if necessary and simplify if at all possible the management structure within your area of responsibility.

2. Make sure you know, and that others know, who is accountable for what tasks, and to whom.

3. Draw up your own Game Plan (see page 130).

This necessitates your identifying and listing task areas down the left-hand column. If you are a production manager, this may entail introducing new products onto the line, which in turn may require training, work study analysis, rate-fixing, a new machine/product flow layout, more staff/less staff, and so on. For a brand manager it might mean introducing a new sales promotion, a money-off say. In turn, this needs feeding in to the packaging design people, production, selling-in to retailers, briefing the sales force, the trade press, the advertising agency, monitoring the success through research, and so on. Then under another task heading the brand manager may be having to organise the sales conference. This will entail fixing dates, finding and booking the venue, briefing an audio-visual company, producing the business and social side of the conference, and all the rest.

Alongside each detailed task put the initials of who is accountable for making it happen, and alongside that who is his or her boss. Finally, list the year out alongside – most organisations work on weeks one to fifty-two, either on a calendar or financial year basis. Ticks, crosses or different coloured stickers should show when each activity is planned to begin, and when it should be completed.

The Game Plan should be kept to one sheet of paper, no matter how big. It can cover an entire wall if necessary. Don't make it look too professional by using Letraset; simply write it out in felt tip pen. It is a living, working planner, not a work of art. What it should convey at a glance is who is responsible for what, and how you are all doing on your targets.

4. Use the Game Plan by writing notes to yourself of things you want to raise with people on the various tasks at appropriate times in the future. Put the notes in envelopes or little plastic folders and stick them on the time-planner chart. Use the Game Plan. Do not rely simply on memory or immediate pressure of work or your key priorities may be lost.

5. Systemise a means to bring people up to date on what is going on – team briefings, or whatever you decide.

6. Make sure you have a method for keeping in touch yourself on a day to day basis. Walk the job, let yourself be seen to be involved at the sharp end. Be accessible. Be seen to be responsible.

7. Establish your own acceptable standards and make people respect them. This means acceptable codes of behaviour covering a whole range of issues like timekeeping, dress, tidiness, grumbling, language, sexism (jokes, girlie calendars, etc), racism, and so on. It is possible to impose your own culture on a group, even if the corporate whole makes no attempt to. We can all recall some of our schoolteachers who, when teaching exactly the same pupils as other teachers, commanded more respect and better behaviour. To borrow from Herman Wouk's *The Caine Mutiny*: there are four ways of doing things on this ship – the right way, the wrong way, the Navy way – and My Way.

8. To achieve this, do it in stages. *The 20% Factor.* Unless you are in a green-field situation, you risk going over the top and being ridiculed if you suddenly started trying to impose a new culture overnight.

9. Keep things simple.

10. All of this will never work until it becomes a drill. Relentlessly stick to your Game Plan and your methodology, insist others do the same. Only when your people realise they *have* to work this way will they do so. People dislike and resist change. They are, however, generally happy to accept clear direction if it makes sense. Don't discuss it. Implement it. Stick to it. The results, the benefits should soon follow. Almost everything at work is measurable. Your problem is to find the measurement.

## The Game Plan

| Task area headings | Who's accountable for task? | Who is their boss? | CALENDAR WEEKS (TO 52) | | | | | | | | | | | | | | | | | | |
|---|---|---|---|---|---|---|---|---|---|---|---|---|---|---|---|---|---|---|---|---|---|
| | | | 1 | 2 | 3 | 4 | 5 | 6 | 7 | 8 | 9 | 10 | 11 | 12 | 13 | 14 | 15 | 16 | 17 | 18 | 19→52 |
| 1 | | | | | | | | | | | | | | | | | | | | | |
| 2 | | | | | | | | | | | | | | | | | | | | | |
| 3 | | | | | | | | | | | | | | | | | | | | | |
| 4 | | | | | | | | | | | | | | | | | | | | | |
| 5 | | | | | | | | | | | | | | | | | | | | | |
| 6 | | | | | | | | | | | | | | | | | | | | | |
| 7 | | | | | | | | | | | | | | | | | | | | | |

## BE MORE PRODUCTIVE

You will see that it is important to discipline yourself, target your real superiors and manage your time in the most focused way possible. As that great time manager Benjamin Franklin said, 'To love life is to love time. Time is the stuff life is made of.'

Time management is so important. It is always easy to fill time and genuinely feel busy. The truth, more often than not however, is that large percentages of that time are being badly used in terms of priorities. Being a busy fool is common enough. We are all tempted to do the easy, pleasant jobs first, and to leave until last the things we least enjoy. To push papers around and not actually do much. To write a letter or memo rather than be more direct and telephone. To wait for others to prompt us to do things we know we should do anyway – like the lazy person lying in bed in the mornings thinking, 'If that alarm doesn't go off soon, I'll be late for work.'

Management expert Peter Drucker has said, 'Effective executives, in my observation, do not start with their tasks. They start with their time. They start by finding out where their time goes. Then they attempt to manage their time and to cut back unproductive demands on their time.'

Once again knowing yourself is the answer. If you're not naturally good at time management and prioritising, become a list maker. List things you have to do that day, that week, then number them in terms of *real* priority (not your own preferences). Make 'have to do', 'ought to do' and 'when I can get round to it' categories. Write them out under these three headings using your Game Plan. At the end of each day or week tick things off. And tick yourself off too, if you're still taking the line of least resistance.

> **❝** *If you have been in the same job for over two years,* **❞**
> *20% of your time should now be free*

The extent to which you may like your boss to see you as conspicuously busy is a moot point. There is a lot of truth in the saying 'if you want a good job doing, ask a busy person'. On the other hand, the most senior people do seem to be much less pestered by a procession of mini-crises and deadlines. They seem more able to be on time for meetings *and* to have read the papers thoroughly beforehand. They seem less likely to be constantly interrupted by urgent-must-take telephone calls when you are in their office and don't have to spend their lives on mobile phones when travelling.

Take your cue from your immediate boss. If he or she is still in the busy-bee phase, then your appearing a serene picture of orderliness and calm will probably be mistaken at best for your not having enough to do, and at worst as some kind of smart-Alec implied criticism of your boss's own ability to manage. Dr Marilyn Davidson, senior lecturer in organisational psychology at UMIST's School of Management says, 'In the office environment you need to look busy. So mess on your desk is a way of saying – look how busy I am.'

However, if your boss takes pride in orderliness (tidy desk tops are the obvious sign) then it is likely that your breathless can't-stop-now routine will be viewed as inexperience or simply plain incompetence. Sir Allen Sheppard, chief executive of Grand Metropolitan has remarked, 'If I saw a mountain of paperwork on someone's desk without any apparent logic I would assume they were out of control.'

Make use of reflective responsing. Reflect back the style and pace of work of your boss.

---

### UNTIDY DESK?

If you are guilt racked about your untidy desk, there is some good news. Dr Mark Lansdale of Loughborough University described the 'volcano model' of paper management to the British Association for the Advancement of Science in 1992.

The volcano model is where you have a mound of papers on your desk with a crater at its centre. New documents come into the crater pushing others to the lip of the volcano to be recovered later, or to be moved 'like a lava flow across the desk before dropping off the edge.'

Dr Lansdale argues that the system is compatible with the way the human memory works and can be perfectly successful. People usually knew where things were.

---

 *20% of an average working day is 96 minutes. Set aside just 20% of this (19 minutes) for a daily self-improvement task*

> ### IS THAT YOUR BEST WORK?
>
> When Dr Henry Kissinger was US Secretary of State he had a shrewd tactic to get the very best out of his people.
> If an aide came to him with a report he would call them back, look them in the eye and ask, 'Is this your best work?' Invariably the aide would blush, take the report back and rework it.
> Dr Kissinger may do the same again with the next report, and perhaps again until the aide confidently said back to him, 'Yes, that *is* my best work.' At which point Dr Kissinger would say, 'Very well. I will now read it.'

## IS IT ETHICAL?

### Morality in Business

*The 20% Factor* is teaching you to show deference, be submissive and to sublimate your individualism. It also recommends that you consider using praise and flattery in a calculated way, along with a host of quasi-psychological techniques.

Some critics will attack this on the grounds that you should assert not hide your individualism; others that 'creeping and crawling' and the use of fake praise is downright unethical. I will look at each criticism in turn.

> ### BLAME JOHN LENNON
>
> In my early twenties I taught young Americans on a summer camp. I remember one describing the real social impact of The Beatles in the early 1960s. Before then, the American middle-class teenage boy had a crew-cut and was an apprentice adult. In terms of dress, behaviour, manners and opinions, his cue was to emulate the values of his parents.
> After The Beatles the scales (already weighed with Presley, Lee Lewis, Dean and Brando) were tipped and longer hair, non-conformist dress and opinions gave American youth its own culture.

### The cult of the individual

For the generation who began work or university in the 1960s and early 1970s, self-expression and individuality were and remain icons. The whole idea of sublimating their character seems unacceptable and wrong.

Many of these – now middle aged people – who today work in the less rigid worlds of entertainment, literature, advertising, journalism, broadcasting, further education, publishing, cinema and the arts, help lead opinion, and can still maintain a degree of cautious Bohemianism in these areas.

In business, however, it is a mistake to try and copy eccentrics or geniuses. If you or I attempt to assert our individualism in the manner of the handful of colourful tycoons that usually come to mind – Iacocca, Harvey Jones, Branson, Perot, Roddick – we would simply look foolish.

In fact this is even true for the arts and showbusiness world. American singer Suzanne Vega, commenting on the Madonna 'wannabes' said, 'All the little girls who like her and dress like her aren't going to grow up rich and famous like her, they're going to grow up to be treated like tramps.

And in a profile on actor Kenneth Branagh, the *Daily Mail* carried the comment 'Very determined people who start with a modest talent become more forceful than those who start with genius.'

In business in particular, bosses and customers want to feel safe if they put us on their corporate mantlepiece. We have to relearn H Gordon Selfridge's famous dictum that the customer is always right – and a customer for your services is also your boss. Find out what they want and present youself as the solution. Highlight a need that you can meet. That is the essence of *The 20% Factor*. Use the existing dynamics of business to your own advantage, as a judo expert uses the size and power of a much bigger opponent to execute a fall.

## Ethics

Rightly or wrongly, most people do not believe that business is at all ethical.

In 1988 the Market Research Society asked a random sample of British people how they rated the standards of honesty of various groups. Twenty nine per cent thought top businesspeople had low standards, with just 17 per cent saying the opposite (the rest had no view).

A survey in 1992, conducted by the Cooperative Bank, of opinion formers suggests that bank managers and personnel executives are thought to be most ethically correct; finance and marketing directors were the least; while doctors, lawyers and journalists occupied the middle ground.

In the USA a Harris Poll for *Business Week* in 1989 asked 'If you had to say, which of the following things do you think business would do in order to obtain greater profits?' The results were:

|  | % |
|---|---|
| Deliberately charge inflated prices | 62 |
| Harm the environment | 47 |
| Knowingly sell inferior products | 44 |
| Put its worker's health/safety at risk | 42 |
| Endanger public health | 38 |
| Sell unsafe products | 37 |

Twenty five per cent of respondents even thought business would do all of these things. Looked at in this light your attempts to put your best face forward seem pretty tame.

The degree to which any individual wishes to use the deliberate manipulation of his or her appearance and personality in the ways I have described is a matter for personal judgement. Some people claim not to have the temperament to bend very far. Others think it is wrong to manipulate social relationships or use their interpersonal skills in this way. Although that is the moot point: you are not manipulating others, only yourself. Not even manipulating – more adapting. As Dr Hans Selye in *Stress Without Distress* says' [the] great capacity for adaption is what makes life possible on all levels ... Adaptability is probably the most distinctive characteristic of life.'

However, moral issues do arise. What if an important customer launches into a racist, sexual or political invective that would get short shrift from you at a purely social gathering? My view would be to absorb the diatribe without comment and rapidly change the subject. Perhaps you would act differently, but I maintain that in most cases that would be wrong. You are representing your *organisation*, not yourself; they would have been reflecting their personal prejudices, not those of their organisation. Let lying dogs sleep.

If, on the other hand, the nature of the company or product with which you are considering becoming involved is offensive to you, then you do of course have the option of declining. For example, over three-quarters of business people surveyed in 1992 said they were opposed to selling weapons to repressive regimes or exporting pesticides banned in the UK.

---

### MORALS – WHAT MORALS?

Some people have a strange view of morality. When working in the holiday industry I once took a call from a man who asked me how far 'far' was. I asked him to explain and he said that he had a holiday brochure which said that a certain hotel was not far from the beach. So how far is 'not far'? Without seeing the brochure in context I said I didn't know, to which he replied that he did. 'Not far' in fact was two kilometres. He knew because he had found the same hotel in another company's brochure giving the distance from the beach. The man proudly told me he was going to book with the operator who said it was 'not far' and, as he suffered from angina, would demand free taxis to and from the beach every day when he got there, plus compensation on his return.

---

*The 20% Factor* is about helping you to meet attainable goals by finding out what people want, and giving it to them. On occasions a price for that is to become a kind of corporate cushion, with you bearing the impression of the last person who sat upon you. Take heart, however. Contrary to popular belief, winners are not leaders, they are the faithful servants of whatever market they are in. The market dictates and winners follow. The most successful people I know – tycoons and others – have a dignified servility for the people and groups important to them that would amaze most of the people who work for them.

## The business of philosophy

I think it is helpful for each of us to have a structure or base on which we build our views on business ethics and morality, and some knowledge of philosophy is useful. For me there are three, sometimes contradictory, strands of philosophical thought behind *The 20% Factor*:

1. Pragmatism, which helps lead towards decisions and actions which will have the desired consequences. Undiluted pragmatism, however, raises the spectre of bribing and corrupting important people to get our way. Even blackmail and murdering competitors! Clearly we need a bridle to ride this safely.

2. The second strand is based on the thoughts of the eighteenth century Prussian philosopher, Immanuel Kant. His dictums

from *Critique of Practical Reason*, published in 1788, were 'Act always to treat humanity whether in your own person or that of any other, always as an end without, and never as a means only' and 'There is nothing in the world, or even out of it, which is unqualifiably good but a good will'.

G E Moore arrived at similar conclusions arguing that it is impossible for moral goodness to exist in any action that is not wholly good in itself. Shakespeare in Hamlet was ahead of them both when he wrote 'Words without thoughts never to heaven go'.

Basically Kant argued that you cannot discuss ethics without considering conscience.

3. The dominant philosophy of business since Victorian times, however, has been Utilitarianism, developed by Jeremy Bentham from his *Principles of Morals and Legislation*, published in 1789. It advocates the greatest happiness for the greatest number as the dominant ideology. It certainly has its critics. Kant for one, with his 'categorical imperative' belief that absolute right should never be modified for the sake of expediency. Today's conviction politician for another and some bosses, military and religious leaders who have their own unshakeable views on what constitutes the 'right' course of action, and will pursue it regardless of consequences. Certainly utilitarianism untouched by that moral imperative has no answer for morality.

Kant would not have approved of *The 20% Factor*, yet I can reconcile my own eclectic business philosophy with his impossibly high moral standards by seeking no more from my methods than the achievement of greater influence and success, which I would hope to use wisely and ethically.

---

## Assess your executive potential ☑

You have now got to know more about yourself as an individual, and as a type of manager. Also you should by now have learned how to understand what your organisation and your immediate boss wants from you.

I have advised you to tailor make your responses in ways that best meet these expectations. Next I want you to evaluate how you rate in terms of executive potential. The following checklist represents criteria which commonly influence how individuals get on in an executive capacity. (Reprinted with permission of Macmillan Publishing Company from *Communicating in Organisations* © 1982 by Gerald M Phillips.)

Those criteria marked with asterisks are areas in which ability to communicate effectively plays an important role. Where you honestly believe you are up to average or above average standard in terms of your own organisation's values, give yourself a single tick. On the starred items, give yourself two ticks.

Score twenty five ticks or more and you are shaping up well for an executive career.

## Job performance

Tick

_____ 1. Performs job as described in the job description without making mistakes

_____ 2. Performs the job on time

_____ 3. Calls the attention of immediate superior to legitimate prob-lems in performing the job and asks guidance if necessary*

_____ 4. Draws attention of immediate superior to problems with other people's work in such a way that unobtrusive corrections are possible*

_____ 5. Avoids talking about personal problems with immediate superiors

_____ 6. Suggests ways to improve and make more effective his or her job as described in the job description

_____ 7. Convinces superiors of ways to save money or speed up work*

_____ 8. Avoids conflict with associates over work

_____ 9. Is able to settle disputes between colleagues*

_____ 10. Collaborates with others to solve problems*

## Personal style

_____ 1. Dresses appropriately for the job

_____ 2. Does not advertise sexuality

_____ 3. Does not conduct personal business on the premises*

_____ 4. Speaks well of colleagues and the organisation

_____ 5. Does not gossip

_____ 6. Does not spread rumours

_____ 7. Does not belong to a political faction in a work sense

_____ 8. Associates generally with the people around him or her

_____ 9. Does not socialise intensely with work colleagues

_____ 10. Supports the organisation's ancillary efforts like charity appeals

## Communications skills at work

_____ 1. Asks useful questions

_____ 2. Answers questions clearly and concisely

_____ 3. Passes on information accurately

_____ 4. Works effectively in problem solving in small groups*

_____ 5. Defends opinions with evidence*

_____ 6. Makes effective public presentations*

_____ 7. Encourages others to work effectively

_____ 8. Shows an understanding of the organisation's objectives

_____ 9. Does not patronise, indulge or insult others

_____ 10. Makes complaints that are justified

_____ TOTAL

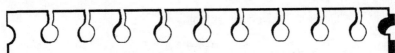

## SUMMARY

Manage for results using *The 20% Factor:*

- Develop your strengths
- Be adept – adapt!
- Be a team player
- Manage your time
- Be approachable, not confrontational.

# 10 BE A 20% BETTER COMMUNICATOR

## WRITING AND SPEAKING – GIFT OR GRAFT?

Let's make one thing clear. Being a good writer and speaking persuasively is not a gift which some people possess and others don't. Becoming competent at both is vital if you are to improve your business performance and – given application – you can become more than competent.

Before giving you some practical guidance on how *The 20% Factor* can improve your writing and speaking, first let us look at the ingredient X which distinguishes pedestrian reports and speeches from memorable ones: *creativity*.

### Creativity

List three or four of the most creative people you can think of – Mozart, Monet, Paul McCartney, Graham Greene perhaps.

The temptation is to believe that creativity is some kind of casual gift possessed by classical and contemporary heroes. Mozart was, after all, a child protégé, wasn't he? And Monet, the father of impressionism, what a clever idea *he* had.

The fact is that creativity is 80 per cent training, discipline, hard work and time, and only perhaps 20% natural bent and talent. Child protégé or not, Mozart had total immersion in music through his father virtually from the cradle, and was exposed to a tremendous variety of musical stimuli in his travels very early on in life around Europe. Monet – already famous at the age of fifteen in his home town of Le Havre for his painting – was nonetheless forced to work with a well-known disciplined teacher, Gleyre. And both he and Pissarro learned a lot from the study of Turner. McCartney's hard apprenticeship with *The Beatles*, playing until he dropped in Hamburg, gave him a training and discipline needed for true popular creativity. As for a master writer like Graham Greene, with over fifty books and plays behind him, he knew that literature was as much about hard work as creativity and flair.

Good ideas, a quick mind, skill at playing clever games with words – these things are not creativity. And the cliché trappings of creative people – moodiness, flamboyant dress and behaviour, being useless at things *practical* – only present a caricature. Creativity, in fact, is simply a form of problem solving, and so identifying the precise problem to be solved is the first and most important step.

If 80 per cent of creativity is preparation and hard work, it follows that people who feel themselves weak creatively can make dramatic improvements in their performance by greater application and method. A good creative director of an advertising agency will expect a very full brief before putting his mind to a solution. He or she will want to immerse themselves in the client's industry, its history, in its production processes, quality control procedures, in its corporate style, in the way customers look at the market – all these things and more before outline creative treatments are drawn up. Once the real creative brief has been thoroughly understood, an acceptable creative solution could become obvious to anyone. The skill is in arriving at that very tight brief.

Creativity in invention and new product development is similar. Most great or useful inventions stem from a need identified by people with a direct interest or knowledge in the subject area – be it digital watches or pot noodles. They know what they are looking for before they begin. Wartime is the biggest hothouse for invention, when the need has lives as well as pound notes attached to it.

To improve your own creative performance:

■ stop trying to search for an answer until you have laboriously defined and refined the question. Spend most of your time on thinking of the objectives and the desired results and responses and at least an acceptable piece of workmanlike 'creativity' will follow – perhaps even better.

■ Give yourself time. One of the greatest failings in so-called uncreative people is this erroneous belief that all that is needed is a bright idea from someone – and that can only take a few minutes. Free-ranging creative brain stormings tend to follow from this and are, on the whole, a bad idea. They are almost always poorly briefed, and people just throw around sparky ideas to show off – whether on strategy or not. If creativity is a form of problem solving, it follows that the ability to implement and follow through proposed solutions must be resolved. Accept that creativity is long, hard work and you will have got over the biggest hurdle.

## IMPROVE YOUR WRITTEN STYLE

Writing falls into much the same category as creativity. Some people hate writing, dread it and are convinced they can never improve. Again, 80 per cent of good writing is preparation, really understanding your audience and objectives, and being prepared to invest the time to draft and re-draft. As for writing well, creatively, most poor writers are convinced that others are born with the knack from birth. Once you believe that, it's easy to become a defeatist and settle for second best. Poor writers also fail to give themselves enough time, believing they need deadlines to write to, like some green eye-shaded hack reporter they have seen in a thirties movie. Of course, the opposite is the truth. Deadlines are the last thing a poor writer needs to reach competence. There is much truth in the old saying 'I'm sorry this letter is so long, but I didn't have the time to write one shorter.'

> **"** *20% of good writing is creativity, the rest is good preparation* **"**

Try the following tips to improve your written style.

### Spelling

For those with a problem with spelling or vocabulary, then a dictionary, word processor spellcheck and Roget's Thesaurus will help. More difficult is a problem with grammar, syntax and punctuation. Some very senior people have had a classical education and have no patience with what they see as elementary mistakes. Split infinitives, the wrong use of who and whom, its and it's, compared 'to' instead of the correct compared 'with', *e*ffect and *a*ffect, 'there are three alternatives' (there can only be two choices in an alternative), the use of crude slang such as 'nitty gritty' – these things can affect the reaction to an otherwise admirable report.

### Know your audience

If your target is pedantic in this respect, play safe. For others a slightly more relaxed style may be acceptable. When writing for most audiences, for example, I will sometimes begin sentences with 'And' or 'But', use split infinitives if not to do so seems contrived, and I do technically misuse colons and semi-colons.

If you have a real problem with your 'it's' or sentence construction, however, you have to accept the need for study and practice. No book of instruction has ever bettered Sir Ernest Gowers' *The Complete Plain Words*, Pelican.

Before you begin writing anything have a very clear idea who is your target audience. What style and length is most appropriate for them? If a report is aimed at very senior management, consider including an executive summary on one double-spaced top sheet. If your audience is the finance director, ensure you support your arguments with accurate costings and forecasts. Senior management in marketing will expect you to display a sensitivity to the effect on market share, key account customers, dealers and retailers, and likely reaction from competitors.

### Presentation

Presentation is important. Double-spacing and wide margins make for easy reading and annotation. Avoid sending facsimile reports and letters to senior people where possible. Standard fax paper is horrible to handle and write upon, and of course it fades. If you *must* fax something, always put a top copy in the post, and say that you have done so on the fax. Always check the fax has been received clearly and politely suggest that it is photocopied and given to the ultimate recipient in that form.

As for the report itself, do ensure that the reader takes from it your indication of what they should do next. Even if you have just prepared background briefing information on which they must come to some executive conclusion, indicate that further information is available from you, and where they can reach you.

In terms of style, formality is always the safe option. Use the third person singular with no use of slang or colloquialisms. Never use office reports to play politics or score points. Memos and reports have a long life and may well be seen by people you did not intend. If you are in any doubt about whether to include somebody in on the 'cc' copy list, then include them. Be transparent. Not being copied, even on innocuous reports to bosses, can easily alienate your immediate superior and peer group.

---

### KEEP SPEECHES SHORT

At one conference a speaker had been speaking for far too long when he said to the delegates, 'I haven't got my watch on, I hope I haven't been going on too long.' A heckler shouted back, 'There's a calendar behind you!'

In the same vein, a famous British ambassador to Washington was fishing for compliments from his wife when returning from a speaking engagement. Wearily she replied that his speech, as ever, put him in the Rolls Royce class. He preened himself and asked what she meant. 'You were well oiled, inaudible and looked as though you could go on forever,' came the frosty reply.

---

I have three additional general tips.

1. Be concise. Few reports suffer from being 20% shorter, and that goes for the length of words used as well as the length of sentences, paragraphs and the total article. Like our letter writer, you will find it can take more time to write a short speech or article than a long one.

2. Before you begin drafting, compose an eight word newspaper-style headline which sums up the most important message you want your reader to remember. You will not use that headline, but once you have finished writing, read it over and see if you really think that message jumps out sufficiently well. If not, it's time for a second or third re-draft.

3. Borrow from the storyteller's craft and give your piece a beginning, a middle and an end. The beginning should attract, surprise and perhaps challenge the reader, to win and hold attention; the middle should inform and develop your argument; and the end should recall the main message – perhaps picking up on a theme from the opening sentence or two.

> **❝** *Cut your report or speech by 20%.* **❞**
> *Few presentations suffer from being 20% shorter*

There follow two examples of some of my own writing to illustrate some of the points I have made. 'The Headhunters' is a short story I wrote for the *Sunday Telegraph Magazine*. I include it, not as a paragon of short story writing (read Maupassant, Somerset Maugham or Capote for that), but as an illustration of how much can be said in a short piece. It is less than 700 words. Whole worlds, places, characters and plot can be created using just a few hundred words; surely we can all convey most pieces of business information no less succinctly.

The first piece, 'Your Service', is even shorter, at just over 500 words. It was one of my regular diary columns for *Marketing* magazine. You will see how I have used a surprising and, I hope, entertaining way to make a serious point about modern service standards in business.

---

### YOUR SERVICE

It's 1959 and I'm sitting in a coffee bar as the jukebox plays Lonnie Donegan, the King of Skiffle. My friends are about to hear my big idea for making my first million when the waitress arrives with another round of Cona coffees and a Penguin each. Yes she can change half a crown, and I give her a tanner tip to show off. She looks like Ruby Murray and my heart flutters.

'Well this is it. My big idea,' say I. 'I'm going to redefine service excellence and start a chain of cafes selling beefburgers.

'So, what's new dadio?' That's my mate Eric, an aspirational beatnik. He's got the sandles, phoney university scarf and a book by Bertrand Russell, but is still saving up for a duffle coat.

'What's new is this,' say I, unruffled by the unduffled. 'You're going to have to queue up to get served. No waitresses. The burgers will be pre-cooked and barely warm. On untoasted baps. With tomato sauce and relish even if you don't want it. And no mustard even if you do. You can have chips, but can't have salt and vinegar. If you want to eat inside, you will have to sit on fixed hard seats which slope down so you don't stay too long. You won't be able to have knives, forks or plates, and will have to eat with your fingers. And then, at the end, you'll have to clear your own table and put the rubbish down a chute. Well? Do you think the public will beat a path to my door?'

Penguins came in thick silver paper in those days and being pelted with wrapper balls was no joke. A visionary could lose an eye. One of my quieter, gentle and more thoughtful friends (strangely he later became a media buyer) asked whether I had conducted any customer sensing research in the sector. But I just fixed him with my Billy Fury narrow-eyed stare. Clint Eastwood stole that stare off Billy and used it in Rawhide years later. But it seems you can't get intellectual copyright on narrow-eyed stares.

'Alright,' said I defiantly. 'I've got another idea to improve service standards. I'm going to invent a machine for use outside banks. They already have night safes for shopkeepers to put money in after hours. Well, I'm going to design a cash dispenser to take your money out. You'll be able to queue outside in the rain instead of inside in the dry, and use your Billy Fury stare to fend off teddy boy muggers with bicycle chains. And you need never see a bank clerk again in your life.'

By now the guys had lost interest. They were laughing at some circus trapeze artist in the Daily Mirror who was predicting that his Hank Marvin lookalike son would one day be prime minister. 'There's about as much chance of that as Hank turning up on your doorstep as a Jehovah's Witness,' scoffed I.

Alright, looking back I can see how wrong I was about John Major and Hank. But I was right about improving service standards, wasn't I? We've gone from the bad old days of Nippies serving hot food on crisp linened tables, and attentive Captain Mainwaring-style bank mangers, to the 1990s Nirvana of Mac-Donalds and First Direct. There's progress for you.

## THE HEADHUNTERS

Henry was excited as he straightened his tie in the bedroom mirror. 'Sharp at ten,' the headhunters had said, and he was determined not to be late. The interview could well be the turning point in his career. Certainly he had long ago come to the decision that he would go no further with his current employers. The Head

Accountant was still in his early fifties; and there could be no promotion other than in dead men's shoes in the small engineering firm's accounts department.

That was why Henry had been so thrilled by the unexpected call a few days earlier. It was from J Paul and Co Ltd, a new firm of executive search and headhunters as they described themselves. Was he happy with his current prospects as *Assistant* Head Accountant? No? Well they had an international client looking for a new Head, and they were offering a car, a guaranteed income of £30,000 for the first year and a ten per cent share of profit from sales revenue directly attributable to his personal contribution. Was he interested in talking?

Naturally Henry had agreed to be discreet about the proposition until all the loose ends had been tied up. He had even agreed to their suggestion not to tell Muriel, his wife. This was not an unusual request from the clients of headhunting firms. They know that the hardest thing on earth is to keep executive searches secret. He had simply told the secretary he shared with the Head Accountant that he would be at the dentist that morning and not to expect him until 11.30am at the earliest.

Muriel commented on his smartness as he went down for breakfast. 'That's your wedding shirt,' she said. 'Got something special on today?' They had been married less than a year.

'Having lunch with the auditors,' he lied.

'I'll just make up a salad for dinner tonight then if you're having a large lunch.'

'Fine, darling.' He was too excited to think about food anyway: £30,000, a car and a share in profits. Not bad for a twenty-six-year-old. How marvellous it would be if he got the job. He would take her out to dinner and tell her that way. It would make such a difference, the extra money. And they could sell the old Austin Mini.

At 9.55am Henry was pressing the bell at the Victorian office block. There was no sign saying J Paul & Co, but he was sure it was the right address.

A porter showed him up to the first floor, knocked gently on the door and left him without speaking. Henry was sweating and he nervously flattened his hair as he waited, wishing he'd had a haircut.

The smooth-looking man who opened the door and ushered him to a chair looked about forty – he was a foreigner, Asian maybe, or perhaps from the Pacific.

'Let's have a drink first,' he smiled genially.

Henry tasted the poison in the coffee, but it made no difference. He was dead within half a minute and laid out ready in the white-tiled cellar in five.

The gleaming new Ford was driven up to Henry's house an hour later. Muriel noticed it when she returned from shopping. When she was inside the house she picked up the envelope. Inside she was surprised to find the car keys and a banker's draft for £30,000 from a numbered Swiss bank account. She was even more surprised when Henry did not come home that night, and devastated when, after a week, the police began to hint gently that they were not optimistic about finding him.

The final link with the mystery came a month later, when the Borneo businessman from J Paul & Co Ltd anonymously sent her a further banker's draft for £25,000, ten per cent of the sale price achieved for the shrunken head. White men's heads fetch the highest prices from collectors in the Middle East and Africa. Henry's fetched a record £250,000.

Report, letter, press release and speech writing is not the same as short story writing – the objectives are very different, one primarily to convey information the other primarily to entertain – but I think the differences can be over-emphasised at the expense of the similarities. To win and retain attention with spoken English, we generally accept the need for an element of entertainment. A certain amount of style and panache, entertainment, can even find its way into business-report writing.

## SPEECH!

I spent almost three years as the speechwriter for the director generals and presidents of the Confederation of British Industry, and I can honestly say that the worst speech I have ever had to sit through was one I wrote myself. It went down well enough on the day and the tycoon who delivered it seemed happy, but its reasonable reception had much more to do with the stature of the man and his office than it did with my over-long, over-ambitious speech.

At the time I was writing an average of three to five speeches *a week* on different topics for different people, at least one or two of which were going to be press-released and possibly recorded for radio and TV.

Most people speak at around 130 words a minute, and they like to ad lib a little, especially at the beginning and the end. I used to estimate a 2500 word speech to be about twenty minutes, 2000 about fifteen. Interestingly, when you write for different people you find yourself having to adopt quite different styles to suit the nature of the people. Of course, all important people write some of their own speeches themselves and parts of others, and none would ever read out something a speechwriter had drafted if he or she did not agree with the content or feel comfortable with the style. On the other hand, beware of the people who say I *always* write my own speeches. *Really* important people are far too busy for that – ask any prime minister or president.

It is a presidential address which is commonly acknowledged to be perhaps the greatest speech in relatively recent history, in terms of literary style and content. It is very short – just 267 words.

The Gettysburg address was delivered in November 1863 by President Abraham Lincoln at the dedication of a cemetery at the Gettysburg battlefield, and it recalled the great principles of equality established by America's founding fathers.

> Fourscore and seven years ago our fathers brought forth on this continent a new nation, conceived in liberty and dedicated to the proposition that all men are created equal.
>
> Now we are engaged in a great civil war, testing whether that nation, or any nation so conceived and so dedicated, can long endure. We are met on a great battlefield of the war. We have come to dedicate a portion of that field as a final resting-place of those who here gave their lives so that the nation might live. It is altogether fitting and proper that we should do this.
>
> But, in a larger sense, we cannot dedicate – we cannot consecrate – we cannot hallow – this ground. The brave men, living and dead, who struggled here, have consecrated it far above our poor power to add or detract. The world will little note, nor long remember, what we say here, but it can never forget what they did here. It is for us the living, rather, to be dedicated here to the unfinished work which they who fought here have thus far so nobly advanced. It is rather for us to be here dedicated to the great task remaining before us – that from these honoured dead we take increased devotion to that cause for which they gave the last full measure of devotion; that we here highly resolve that these dead

shall not have died in vain; that this nation, under God, shall have a new birth of freedom, and that government of the people, by the people, for the people, shall not perish from the earth.

A speech to a trade association or sales conference may seem pretty far removed from the Gettysburg address – but again the similarities are stronger than the obvious differences. Brevity, knowing your audience, having a message and delivering it with style, memorably, should be features shared by all speeches and speakers.

Remember the beginning, middle and end requirement. Remember your need to fine tune the objectives of the speech – and of the organisers in asking you. Remember that most speeches can be shortened to good effect. Time yourself, and make allowances for the fact that you will probably talk a little faster on the day. Also practise your method of delivery. Don't wave your arms about or modulate your voice like some bad Victorian actor playing melodrama – but do use visual and voice emphasis to introduce pace and variation. Otherwise you drone and bore.

Humour should be left to the experienced speaker, unless you have one or two (no more) very safe in-jokes for your audience, best when directed at yourself.

Many people recommend inexperienced speakers to use cards to fit into the palm of your hand containing just headings to prompt you. Don't ever *read* a speech they warn. I disagree with this, and even though I am now an experienced public speaker, I still quite often use fully written-out speeches. In practice I do use them as prompts, but see nothing wrong in reading either, so long as you keep good eye contact with the audience. For inexperienced speakers I certainly recommend it, for its placebo effect alone. Any questions and answers, of course, are off the cuff, but rehearsed and anticipated.

With good preparation and rehearsal, you should never really fail. After all, they have asked you or your organisation to speak in the first place.

One definition of an expert is someone who knows marginally more than his or her audience. Be confident, especially during questions. You know much more about your subject than you think you do. After all, you spend most of your waking hours through the week devoted to it.

If you are making a speech, your throat dries up and you lose the power to speak for fear of uncontrollable coughing or choking (it's happened to me), don't grab a glass of water. The live TV and radio broadcasters' advice is to pause and let your saliva gather to lubricate your throat. It is far more effective than water which, ironically, washes saliva away temporarily leaving you even worse off. You will feel as though such a pause is an eternity, but it should be no more than fifteen to thirty seconds at most. My advice is to pause, take a glass of water and pretend to drink from it, in order to fill the time and relax the audience, who will have noticed the frog in your throat becoming worse.

As for speaking at small formal or informal meetings, where you feel the need to impress or hold your own, the best advice is to take your time. In all groups a natural leader will surface to drive the meeting forward and fill awkward gaps. Let someone else fill that high risk role. Meanwhile keep your body language and eye contact in attentive mode, pre-plan one or two sensible points you want to make (you probably have no more than that anyway) and seize your opportunity to make them. If you have not been hogging the discussion, the group will want you to join in and will make it easy for you. Speaking softly when you have the floor is a tactic used by some – often women – to command full attention.

Never show any other emotion than enthusiasm in meetings, and if you really have to disassociate yourself with something that has been said, or the direction the meeting is going, do so succinctly and with no hint of destructive criticism.

Decide who you want to influence and address in the meeting before it begins, and try and sit opposite them in order to be able to use your body language and eye contact skills to full effect and to each of them.

Finally, as in so many aspects of life and art, editing is the key. The things you *don't* say and a period of attentive silence from you can have just as much impact as your short, to the point and hopefully pre-rehearsed contribution. Remember what we discussed earlier about being a good, supportive listener. If you can send supportive signals to your target in the meeting when they are speaking, you will be surprised afterwards at how well they thought you performed – even if you never opened your mouth.

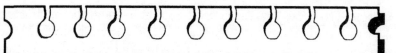

## SUMMARY

Only 20% of creativity is natural talent, the rest is hard work and preparation, so remember to:

■ Know your audience and what they want from you

■ Brush up on your grammar

■ Be concise

■ Practise presentation skills.

# PART 3 CHECKLIST

- Happiness and success come from shared – personal and organisational – values and goals

- Imagine companies as individuals; don't generalise

- Regular praise and recognition at all levels improves morale, motivation and therefore success

- Learn to listen, not just hear

- A good corporate image occurs when target audience needs are being anticipated and met

- Self-assessment of yourself and your team will help you discover and adjust strengths and weaknesses

- 80 per cent of good writing is preparation and understanding your target audience and objectives

- Creativity has surprisingly little to do with natural talent – more with discipline and hard work

- Keep speeches and reports brief, stylish and memorable

- Don't be afraid to flatter and praise in business

- Highlight your customer's needs and aim to satisfy them

- Winners are faithful servants, not leaders

# WIN WITH THE

# 20%

# FACTOR

Becoming aware of your areas of potential and weakness, and working steadily towards self-improvement has been the chief aim of *The 20% Factor*.

Turning this awareness into action, with practical guidance on how to do this, has been our parallel theme.

Part 4 summarises the concept of *The 20% Factor* and how it can help you attain achievable business goals and self-fulfilment.

# 11 HAVE I GOT THERE?

*4 x 20% improvements equals an increase in performance potential of over 100% on your original starting point*

I said in the introduction to this book that you should not aim to be a managerial superstar, a top tycoon, because this was too ambitious a target for most of us.

Human nature is such that despite this, most people do have a belief that they could be a top boss given the right breaks. I think this is a false and dangerous assumption, and for this reason believe the vast majority of people should put the idea firmly out of their mind.

If nepotism and hereditary management dynasties are ignored, the common ingredients of the entrepreneurs and professional management tycoons are, frankly, off-putting for most people. As the Robert Half survey into senior management success makes clear, far and away the most important requirement is sheer determination. Single-minded determination and hard work – six or seven days a week of twelve hour plus days – is what is needed. This is common both to entrepreneurs who start up, buy and sell businesses, and to the professional salaried top managers who are equally at home running any one of the multinationals anywhere in the world.

A survey conducted by *The Mail on Sunday* Money Analysis team into senior management in 1992 gives an insight into life at the very top. It shows they are almost twice as likely to divorce as senior management one tier lower and suggests a breed of people who lead irrational lives – confirmed workaholics who sleep little. As marriage, parental or social partners they seem sad characters, suffering from the corporate tunnel vision needed to succeed. Some other characteristics suggest a degree of childhood adversity, with top bosses more likely to have lost a parent in early childhood, had a domineering mother and to have had disadvantaged social origins – such as immigrants or those from poor backgrounds who mixed with children from a higher class.

Sir John Harvey Jones, the former chairman of ICI says, 'The ones who make it are hungrier and greedier for power than the rest.' More ominously psychotherapist Michelle Charrey, who wrote the bestseller *Le Golden Stress* senses that some tycoons are emotionally disturbed and that work is a way for them to fight off depression. My own experience of tycoons supports this. Whereas there are, of course, many urbane, charming and perfectly well-balanced captains of industry, I have seen some display disturbing characteristics of mild paranoia through bouts of fiery temper, irrational pet likes and dislikes and hatred for certain analysts, journalists or competitors.

These are largely salaried people. Owner managers have different characteristics. The successful entrepreneur is a rare and frequently obnoxious individual. Think hard before you aspire to become one yourself. Picture the shops that spring up in most small town High Streets from time to time selling stuffed toys and handcrafted goods. They always seem to have clever sounding names – long agonised over – with beautiful signs and stationery.

You see their eager proprietors rearranging their lovely window displays. But nobody goes in – or if they do they just browse. The owners put on a brave face, opening at 9.00 sharp each morning, six days a week until the dream bursts and the bank calls in the debt.

The true entrepreneur would probably never have been in that business in the first place, and even if he or she had they would have imported from Taiwan and supplied big department stores. The true entrepreneur would have had a tiny office off the expensive High Street, and they would not have agonised over a name – they would have bought a shelf company for a fraction of the cost.

---

### 'I MAKE MONEY'

I once asked an entrepreneurial boss of a small clothing company what he made – meaning raincoats, suits, dressing gowns or whatever. He answered by saying he 'made money' – by going after whatever profitable market opportunity he could identify be it Davy Crockett hats, hot pants, leg warmers or SAS balaclavas.

Largely, I think, because of over-specialism in management, this kind of thinking is now seemingly too abstract for most salaried managers.

Most people are not cut out to start businesses, or to go in and turn problem companies around. Their main burning drives are procreational or recreational. They want job satisfaction, peer group recognition and status, and a competitive remuneration package. On the other hand they probably obtain much less *real* satisfaction from the fruit of their labours than from the fruit of their loins or the end of a fishing rod or tennis racket. This is how it should be and is *not* something to regret.

*The 20% Factor* is designed progressively to improve:

- peer group status
- remuneration package
- business and
- social life

consistent with a more satisfying, holistic outlook on life.

# 12 THE 20% FACTOR: FROM COUÉ TO CARNEGIE

Success on many levels – personal and corporate – is in our own hands. *The 20% Factor* aims to help you achieve that success steadily and effectively.

As important as learning about self-improvement has been our need to 'unlearn' some of the influences of the past quarter of a century – the blind worship and attempted emulation of the *images* we have of heroes from the worlds of business and entertainment; the 1960s attempts to canonise the importance of individuality and to exercise an almost constitutional right to self-expression; the 'go for gold'/'go for it' mentality glibly promoted by the talented, privileged or lucky few.

In their place I have, throughout this book, advocated sets of values which were commonly accepted until the late 1950s, values to which new generations have never been fairly exposed, and against which my own has been poisoned. Values which include the study of others, the sublimation of some of our individuality, the use of self-interested servility, and the embracement of unfashionable clichés like 'the customer is always right' and 'Heaven helps those who help themselves'.

> *Take up 20% of slack and you'll find that another 20% becomes possible*

I believe the advice I have given can lead quickly to a much greater sense of fulfilment, the achievement of sensible goals and the rediscovery of fun and happiness in personal and corporate life to replace the designer boredom and cynicism of the 1980s and early 90s. Much of the unhappiness we see around us arises from feelings of failure and rejection by people exposed to images of apparent success on TV, in magazines and other media, of smiling, self-satisfied 'winners'.

By improving ourselves by 20%, by reaching this attainable new plateau, and then after a while by ratcheting up a further twenty, and then later another twenty, we too can become winners by our own and anybody else's definition.

My advice to reject much of today's accepted wisdom seems radical. It does seem radical to reject the cult of individualism for conformity. It does seem radical to counsel against copying business superstars – pursuing excellence and going for the 'burn'. The fact is, however, that none of this is the least bit radical. Quite the reverse – until recently it was conventional thinking. Conventional thinking deeply rooted in philosophy and practical application. The real shock, I find, is how rapidly and thoroughly these self-evident truths became discredited following that now discredited decade of the 1960s.

---

### IN PURSUIT OF MEDIOCRITY?

It is common in our social lives to try and emulate our heroes.

Socially I envy the great raconteurs like Peter Ustinov, wish I looked as good as 007 in a dinner jacket, could drive off the tee like Faldo and was as sickeningly good at just about everything as Dudley Moore. Realistically, of course, I adjust my sights. I have a half dozen reliable after-dinner stories which seem to work; I may seem more like a waiter than James Bond, but I look OK in a dark corner of The Dorchester in my consommé-stained tux; I occasionally hook my slice to produce a straight drive; and I can casually tinkle a little Cole Porter and finish before anyone notices that I never touch a black note on the piano.

If we all cope socially this way with our lot, why is it so many people convince themselves they can run great businesses better than anyone already doing so? I think part of the blame has been the rash of best selling 'look at me, Ma' books over recent years from tycoons and their ghost writers. Some of these books can seriously damage your career.

Four very different examples follow of what, for most of this century has been – and to me still remains – valuable conventional thinking: Smiles, James, Coué and Carnegie.

The first bestseller on self-improvement was a book called *Self Help*, published in 1859. It was written by doctor and journalist Samuel Smiles, and sold over 250,000 copies during his lifetime. It dealt with the benefits of thrift, temperance, work and good character. In *Self Help* Smiles wrote:

> The spirit of self-help is the root of all genuine growth in the individual; and, exhibited in the lives of many, it constitutes the true source of national vigour and strength. Help from without is often enfeebling in its effects, but help from within invariably invigorates...
>
> The instances of men in this country who, by dint of persevering application and energy, have raised themselves from the humblest ranks of industry to eminent positions of usefulness and influence in society, are indeed so numerous that they have long ceased to be regarded as exceptional. Looking at some of the more remarkable instances, it might almost be said that early encounter with difficulty and adverse circumstances was the necessary and indispensable condition of success.

Psychologist and philosopher William James was one of the founders of pragmatism and, incidentally, the brother of novelist and essayist Henry James. Initially trained as a doctor, he later turned from physiology to psychology and philosophy, initially drawing from Darwin, emphasising the complementary functioning of both the biological and philosophical side of the mind. He went on to argue what lies at the heart of *The 20% Factor* – that we make use of only a small part of our physical and mental resources, that we live far within our limits.

From the same era, the turn of the nineteenth century, came another medically trained man who also made the link between the natural sciences and philosophy. Frenchman Emile Coué, a pharmacist, developed a theory of healing based on auto-suggestion – 'Self-Mastery Through Conscious Auto-Suggestion'. He lectured in Canada and the USA towards the end of his life in 1922 and 1923, when his system had become known as Couéism.

Couéism gave us one of the sickliest sounding pieces of advice of all time, and it jars today more than ever before. Yet it is another cliché that we ignore to our cost. Coué taught his patients to think and say to themselves over and over again – 'Every day in every way, I am getting better and better'. Try saying that out loud today in the pub or in the office and you would be ridiculed.

Steady, measured self-improvement is far from ridiculous however. Believe you can get a little better, believe in *The 20% Factor* – but don't say it out loud. You don't need a soapbox to win conviction. *Private* conviction is what works. We are our own hardest taskmasters. We are our own cathedrals. We can ask and expect more of ourselves than anyone else.

Ten years after the death of Coué came the publication of one of the most influential popular books of this century, a seminal work in the area of applied human relations and one never bettered. It is *How to Win Friends and Influence People*, written by Dale Carnegie. Carnegie was driven to write the book following a survey conducted by the University of Chicago and the United YMCA Schools. It asked the people of a typical American town – Meriden, Connecticut – about themselves, what interested them and what subject areas they would most like to study. Health was the first unsurprising choice for the adults in the survey. Little change there from today, and little change on their second choice. It was how to understand and get on better with people.

Surprisingly, there was no practical textbook covering this subject and Dale Carnegie decided to write his own to use on his courses. This desire to improve ourselves and to improve our relations with others is just as strong today as in the days of Coué and Carnegie.

The myth of the overnight sensation, of bursting suddenly from a chrysalis, of striking it rich, getting lucky, has surely been discredited by experience. The only sure way of making money out of gold prospecting is to sell picks and pans to the hopefuls. Waiting for your luck to change in life is a loser's easy way out – when it does not arrive just blame Lady Luck, not yourself.

Most successful people – people on the national scene or in your own circle of acquaintances – have taken years to get there, years to develop their presentational and interpersonal skills. We notice them *arriving* – we tend to forget how long it took for them to get there.

Success is what we make of it. Improve your understanding and performance in the ways described and take up that first 20%. It will not only help you achieve a greater degree of success, it can be the key to some things which success and fulfilment are really about, but which remain as elusive as ever to some of the be-knighted, ennobled and fawned over stars of business, entertainment and politics: the 'small' matters of contentment, self-respect and happiness.

Only fools and geniuses look for overnight success, and most of us are neither.

20%

# QUARTERLY CHECKLIST

Don't finish reading *The 20% Factor* and put it away on the bookshelf.

I'm urging you to improve yourself *progressively*, so you'll need to do periodic checks on some of the fundamentals we've discussed.

Skim read the book again in a month and use a marker pen to highlight *20% Factor* tips that you find most relevant. Make your own list of them. Photocopy it and keep a copy in your desk.

Then, once a quarter, run over this short checklist to keep *The 20% Factor* method to the fore.

Tick where you feel you have made a 20% improvement in the areas listed on the following pages.

# CHECK-OUT YOURSELF ☑

Have you made a 20% improvement in any or all of these areas?
If so, tick the box.
*How do I seem to my boss/customers?*

- First impressions ☐
- Dress sense ☐
- Hair/grooming ☐
- Size (fat, thin) and health ☐
- Energy level (enthusiastic, laid back) ☐
- Do I defer in terms of attitude? ☐
- Am I using body language effectively? ☐
- Can I now use reflective responsing skilfully? ☐
- Have my written and oral skills improved? ☐
- Do I manage my time well? ☐
- Have I avoided embarrassing crises? ☐

# CHECK-OUT YOUR ORGANISATION ☑

Do my strengths match those of my organisation?

- Do I fit in? ☐
- Have I changed my management style to better match the company culture? ☐
- Do I really know who (or what) will influence my immediate chances of success? ☐
- Do I give that person what I know they look for? ☐
- Have I been able to make influential people like me? ☐
- Am I becoming better at getting what I want from meetings? ☐
- Am I being too impatient/overambitious? ☐

List five areas where you most need to improve by 20 per cent. Concentrate on them for the next quarter, then review your progress again:

1. ............................................................................................................

2. ............................................................................................................

3. ............................................................................................................

4. ............................................................................................................

5. ............................................................................................................

20%

# INDEX